SAFE MONEY MINDSET

A DIFFERENT WAY OF LOOKING AT MONEY SO YOU DON'T RUN OUT IN RETIREMENT

By Jeff Perry
With Contributions by Gene Wittstock

This booklet discusses general concepts for retirement income planning and is not intended to provide tax or legal advice. Individuals are urged to consult with their tax and legal professionals regarding these issues.

The stories and characters in this book are fictional. Each story combines facts and circumstances redacted to highlight the subject matter of each chapter. Facts and circumstances are fictional and do not represent any one client in part or whole. They are included as educational tools. No story should be treated to apply to the reader's individual circumstances. Always consult with your tax professional, attorney, and adviser before taking any action.

Investment advisory services offered through Foundations Investment Advisers, LLC, an SEC registered investment adviser. The content provided is intended for informational and educational purposes only. The views, statements and opinions expressed herein are those of the individual speaker(s) and not necessarily those of Foundations and its affiliates.

Any comments regarding safe and secure investments and guaranteed income streams refer only to fixed insurance products. They do not in any way refer to investment advisory products. Rates and guarantees provided by insurance products and annuities are subject to the financial strength of the issuing insurance company; not guaranteed by any bank or the FDIC. A Roth conversion may not be suitable for your situation. The primary goal in converting retirement assets into a Roth IRA is to reduce the future tax liability on the distributions you take in retirement, or on the distributions of your beneficiaries. The information provided is to help you determine whether or not a Roth IRA conversion may be appropriate for your particular circumstances. Please review your retirement savings, tax, and legacy planning strategies with your legal/tax advisor to be sure a Roth IRA conversion fits into your planning strategies.

Gene Wittsock is not an Investment Adviser Representative of Foundations and does not provide advisory services. Quest Commonwealth does have Jeff Perry, a Foundations investment adviser that can provide such services.

Copyright © 2024 by Magellan Financial, Jeff Perry and Gene Wittstock. Co-authored and edited by Carol Jean Butler. All rights reserved. No part of this publication may be reproduced, distributed, or transmitted in any form or by any means, electronic or mechanical, including photocopying, recording, or by any information storage and retrieval system, without written permission of the publisher, except in the case of brief quotations embodied in critical reviews and certain other noncommercial uses permitted by copyright law.

Printed in the United States of America
First Printing, 2024
Cover and interior design by the Magellan Creative Team

TABLE OF CONTENTS

PROLOGUE .... **VII**
FEAR IN RETIREMENT

INTRODUCTION: **1**
THE WOMEN WHO STARTED IT ALL

What Everybody Wants and Why They Can't Get It 3

The Quest Continued 5

A New Way of Thinking About Money 6

STEP 1 .... **11**
UNDERSTAND WHAT GOT YOU HERE AND WHERE YOU'RE GOING NEXT

What Nobody Is Telling You 13

    What You Did & Why It Works 16

    What You Need To Do Now 17

Your 3 Financial Phases 20

A Take-Action Kind of Guy 24

STEP 2 .... **31**
IDENTIFY YOUR 5 BIGGEST THREATS

Risk #1: Taxes 35

Risk #2: Market Risk 37

Risk #3: Inflation 42

Risk #4: Long-term Care or Future Healthcare 44

Risk #5: Death of a Spouse 47

What 20-Year Period Are You Retiring In? 49

STEP 3 55
UTILIZE THE THREE WORLDS OF MONEY

How To Evaluate Your Investments 58
    Safety 59
    Liquidity 60
    Return 62

THE 3 WORLDS OF MONEY 63

World A: Protection 65
    Fixed Annuity 66
    Money Market Accounts 67
    Bank CD 67

World B: Potential 69
    Stocks 70
    Investment Funds 72
    Bonds 74
    Variable annuity 76

World C: Hybrid 77
    Fixed-Indexed Annuity 78
    Indexed Universal Life 79

How Much Should You Put in Each World? 81

STEP 4 87
CHOOSE THE RIGHT VEHICLE FOR THE JOB

Identify Your Income Gap 90
Fill Your Income Gap 93
Spiders & Annuities: Why People Hate Them 94
How to Choose the Right Vehicle for the Job 96
    When do you need the income? 96
    Immediate Annuities 97
    Deferred Annuities 98
    A Brief Argument About Annuities 99

What the fixed-index annuity can do 100
Why Zero is Your Hero 102

STEP 5 109
CONSIDER FUTURE TAX OBLIGATIONS
The Ticking Tax Time Bomb 112
THE 3 WORLDS OF TAXES 117
    The Taxable World 117
    The Tax-deferred World 118
    The Tax-free World 119
The Window of Tax Opportunity 121
    Take The Reins From The IRS 123
Rules Of The Roth 127
    What About Your Family? 129

STEP 6 135
BREAK UP WITH YOUR CURRENT ADVISER
Get Advice That Is For *You* 140
The Broker VS. The Fiduciary 143
Continue The Quest 145

EPILOGUE 149
ABOUT THE AUTHOR 153
GENE WITTSTOCK 155
GLOSSARY OF TERMS 159

PROLOGUE

FEAR IN RETIREMENT

*"I am the master of my fate.
I am the captain of my soul."*

~William Ernest Henley

This is not your typical retirement planning book. I am not your average adviser. I am a man on a quest. A frustrated, dissatisfied, persistent man who during the peak of his career found out that his wife had lost her job, and so I went looking for some comprehensive financial planning advice.

And I couldn't find any.

Since that time, I have been on a journey—there and back again. What I found was an industry fraught with discrepancies, a lack of education, a lack of transparency, and, in some cases, total and intentional deception. This got me angry. People like me who had worked a lifetime to *save* the money had no idea what they needed to *do* with the money once it came time to prepare for retirement. We continue plodding along in the same old investments, hoping and praying that these die-at-your-desk retirement plans would somehow function when we needed them to. Only, for my wife and I, the time of retirement had come up way earlier than expected, and we needed to know what to do *now*.

I kept making calls, setting up meetings, talking with the HR department where she worked. I sat down with advisers and fund managers at the big corporations whose names you would recognize, but I won't name names in this book. They offered me pie charts, templates, and five-sentence questionnaires. They offered me one-size-fits-all solutions to my risk tolerance and the situation of my wife's early retirement. Nothing about a 30-year timeline, rising taxes, sinking markets, rampant inflation, or life insurance.

Nothing about us as living, breathing people.

I was looking for *real retirement planning* and just not finding it. I thought, *there has got to be somebody out there who knows how to do this right.*

Then, one day, I met with Gene Wittstock.

Now, I'm a decisions guy. When I heard Gene talk about the *Three Worlds of Money*, I knew this was what I'd been looking for. I'd never seen anything like it before. It's not super complicated or groundbreaking, but that's the beauty of it—anyone can understand it. It functions, it makes sense, and it prepares you for the realities of retirement today.

Three meetings later, my wife and I were done, and we had a true plan in place that would see both of us *to* and *through* retirement. But I couldn't stop thinking about all the people I knew who would be facing these decisions next. The experience of that search never left me. Gene and I continued to have conversations.

The rest, as they say, is history.

Today, I am an investment adviser representative. I ended up leaving my job, abandoning my career, and coming onboard with Gene. I am now on a mission to help serve his clients and get this education out there. That's why I'm so different from every other adviser. I'm coming at this to you from the perspective of the client.

This is the book I was looking for when I was in your shoes.

INTRODUCTION:

THE WOMEN WHO STARTED IT ALL

*"Do not go where the path may lead.
Go instead where there is no path
and leave a trail."*

~Ralph Waldo Emerson

To illustrate why retirement planning has gotten so complicated, let me tell you a little story about our firm's founder and CEO, Gene Wittstock. As a first-generation immigrant from Poland, Gene doesn't like to brag. He's shy about going on camera and doing television shows and podcasts, but I'm not, so I'm going to broadcast this story for him.

After leaving his home country of Poland due to opposing political beliefs over communism, Gene landed in Michigan with 20 dollars in his pocket and a passion to engage in the rich culture of Detroit. Working as a laborer, he paid his way through school, graduated with honors from William Tyndale College, and earned a Master of Finance degree. When he first started out in his career as an adviser, he worked for a prestigious brokerage house.

He didn't have a rolodex of contacts, so he started by meeting with a handful of women who lived in Detroit and didn't know how to save for retirement.

These women were all hardworking and many of them were also raising families. He met with them in person and took the time to educate them about their allocation options. He showed them what to do and how to invest, and they made their own choices about how to take what little money they had to save and invest for their futures.

These women trusted him. They were living in the city on their own, and some of them were also single parents. The money that they invested was everything they had in the world, and Gene understood this and took his job seriously.

Word spread. These women recommended Gene's services to their family and friends. He was really trying to take care of people, he got a reputation, and things were going well. The markets were rising, accounts were growing, and his practice was building. He felt good about the services he was able to provide.

Then, in March of 2000, everything changed. The market started losing money. On April 14, the Nasdaq fell by nearly 10 percent, its second-biggest single-day plunge at that time.[1]

In 2001, the market lost again.

In 2002, the market lost again.

---

[1] Baker, Brian, Biggest Stock Market Crashes in History, Bankrate, September 2023, https://www.bankrate.com/investing/biggest-stock-market-crashes-in-us-history/ Accessed 10/05/2023.

By October of 2002, the market had bottomed out, and the Nasdaq had lost nearly 80 percent of its value.[2]

Gene was living in a constant state of panic. He felt deeply responsible for these women. They had made sacrifices and gone without so they could follow his advice and save for retirement, and now they were losing money they couldn't afford to lose. He felt it was his directive to make sure they were okay. He needed to find a way to keep their money safe.

Gene went on a quest looking for safe money strategies. He did the research, looking for an alternative to the stock market, a place that would protect a nest egg and keep it safe from loss.

What he found wasn't taught to him in books or classes. Gene had a master's in finance, six years of education, and yet, no one at any time had ever taught him anything about safe money strategies. It was either economics or the stock market, Wall Street or the bank. He had to learn about safe money options through self-study.

His research paid off. Gene found the perfect solution. He knew exactly what he wanted to get for his loyal ladies.

WHAT EVERYBODY WANTS AND WHY THEY CAN'T GET IT

Once he discovered the solution, Gene was eager to get his ladies into these safer vehicles. He set up a meeting with his boss. He presented the findings of all his research and explained how these innovative solutions worked.

---

[2] Ibid.

"This is what everybody is looking for," he said. "It's what we all need and want!"

"Sorry," his boss told him. "We can't offer that."

Gene was shocked.

"Why not?"

"We can't get it."

"What do you mean?"

"It's not on the menu."

"Will it ever be on the menu?"

"I'm afraid not."

The investment firm where he worked simply didn't have access to these products and strategies.

Gene left that meeting distraught. He had found the solution, but his brokerage house didn't offer the product. He couldn't leave these women in the market after what he had just seen. Gene didn't know what he was going to do. These ladies had entrusted their money to him. They had followed his recommendations and done everything right. That meant something to him. He felt it was his duty to take care of them.

Gene did the only thing he could think to do that would give him peace of mind.

He quit the brokerage firm.

The only way to get these women into the safe money strategies they deserved was to go out on his own as an independent agent. As an independent agent, Gene was able to offer his clients *anything* from the menu of financial products and strategies—it didn't matter what it was; what mattered was that it solved their problems and served them best. And that is exactly what he did.

Gene went out on his own and, one by one, he signed up his ladies for a safe money strategy designed for them. The core group of women who had come to trust Gene followed his advice. He kept their business as he in turn took care of them, making sure they never had to lose money to the market again.

Along came the Great Recession of 2008.

Everybody on Wall Street lost money. Everybody *except* the women that Gene had taken care of. They had gotten into a safe-money strategy, and so their retirement income was not affected. None of their accounts lost a single dime due to market fluctuations in 2008.

For a time, this strategy worked well. Gene was so shellshocked by those years of market loss; he left behind the world of securities and didn't want anything to do with market investments again. But he knew he couldn't do this forever. He understood he couldn't put 100 percent of his clients' money there—retirement today can last 20 to 30 years with the threat of inflation always on the horizon along with the rising cost of healthcare.

In 2009, the markets started rising. Now was the time to get back in. Gene would tell people, "Take the rest of your savings and go talk to someone else." But then he would worry about them—were they paying high fees? Managing their risk? Getting hit by loss at the wrong time?

THE QUEST CONTINUED

Macomb County, Michigan, is home of the automobile industry giants—Ford Motor Company and General Motors to name just a few. One day through a mutual friend, Gene met an elected commissioner named Bill Revoir who was in charge of managing an $800 million pension fund. Bill had been licensed in securities since the 1970s, and the two of them hit it off immediately. Their partnership started when Gene admitted he was open to offering securities again, if only he could find the right fund manager.

"What are you looking for?" Bill asked.

"A money manager who didn't lose any money in 2008."

While that sounded impossible, Bill knew a lot of different money managers around the country because of his experience on the pension board. Gene interviewed them personally, going down the list.

One day, he found his guy.

In 2009, Gene brought him onboard and founded a new firm called Quest Financial. This was an independent financial planning firm capable of offering both safe money solutions *and* tactically managed money. I'm happy to report that the firm is still alive and well today. It has been rebranded to Quest Commonwealth, and our team of fiduciary advisers—myself included—is growing strong. Bill and that money manager are still with the firm.

So are the ladies from Detroit.

A NEW WAY OF THINKING ABOUT MONEY

Everybody knows they need some amount of safe money. We all know this! The majority of people today are living longer and retiring with fewer sources of guaranteed income. Instead of receiving Social Security for two to three years, we are receiving it for 20. Instead of receiving pensions, we are investing in retirement accounts like the

401(k). Corporations are saving trillions because they don't have to manage this pension money anymore.

Instead, *you* have to manage it.

If you are relying on a 401(k), IRA, 403(b), 457, or money in a Thrift Savings Plan, then guess what? You are invested 100 percent in market risk.

If you are putting 100 percent of your money in the stock market, no one can promise that you won't lose this money.

Statistics tell us that market corrections with declines between 10 and 20 percent happen every two years on average.[3] The average length of retirement today—20 years. How will you weather these setbacks?

Pension funds are managed by some of the brightest economic minds in the country. Who is managing your 401(k) or IRA money? I'm willing to bet it's not the top minds in the country; it's you. Which begs the question: *Do you have any training in this area?*

Whether you have saved $100,000 or $12 million, everyone needs to make allocation decisions about how to protect this money. Just investing the way that you've always done and earning a high return isn't enough to retire on today! If you get nothing else from reading this book, please know this:

Investing in retirement isn't just about getting the money to grow; it's about getting the money to last.

---

[3] Guggenheim Investments, Putting Pullbacks in Perspective—White Paper, Summer 2023, https://www.guggenheiminvestments.com/advisor-resources/crucial-conversations-client-facing Accessed 10/06/2023.

If you can understand this, then you can achieve a holistic plan. This plan must consider the five areas outlined in this book: income, investments, taxes, healthcare, and legacy. This plan must properly allocate your portfolio into the *Three Worlds of Money*. This plan must give you an amount of safe money.

There is a big change coming once you retire. With this change needs to come a new way of thinking. Everybody knows they need some amount of safe money. What they don't know is how to change their thinking to get that.

There are six steps you can take to change the way you manage your investments in retirement, and these six steps are outlined in this book. Yes, you can stay invested during retirement. Yes, you can get an income that you won't outlive. This book will show you how to invest with a safe money mindset so that you can retire with confidence and enjoy the rest of your life.

~ Jeff Perry, Investment Adviser Representative and Chief Marketing Officer of Quest Commonwealth, a full-service financial planning firm serving residents of Michigan and beyond.

STEP 1

UNDERSTAND WHAT GOT YOU HERE AND WHERE YOU'RE GOING NEXT

*"When you fail to plan,
you are planning to fail."*

~ Benjamin Franklin

My wife, Medina, likes to help people. If I only say one thing about her, it's that she's the absolute nicest human being you will ever meet. You're going to think it's fake, she's so nice. But it's not! She just really likes helping other people.

The year was 2017, Medina was working in downtown Detroit, and her office was in a big high-rise. Her commute was only fifteen minutes, and she loved the hustle and bustle of working downtown: the whoosh of the cars going by in the busy city streets and making friends with the homeless people. She had one guy who she checked up on, giving him hats and gloves. She eventually helped him to find a shelter so he could get an address and a job—yes, she really did this.

Her job with AT&T also involved helping people. She worked as second-tier support crew for the overseas call centers where she helped people get their problems solved. But the company was always trying to cut back, especially in the Midwest where they were heavily unionized with the highest-paying jobs. Because it was possible to hire people from the South for half the money, this was always a constant threat. That year, Medina's office was surplussed: they had too many people for the jobs at hand.

Suddenly, everything about our future became uncertain.

Medina had been working with AT&T for 27 years. After laying off the bottom 10 people, the company was giving the rest of their employees the option of either moving to a different office with a different job function or taking an early retirement with a buyout.

If she stayed with the company, Medina would have to commute to the northern suburbs an hour away. Her job would also change to a new function. Instead of *helping* people, she would be *selling products* to them. She didn't like the sound of that.

She came to me.

"Can we afford for me to retire early?" She wanted to know.

At the time, I was managing commercial television programming for one of the largest pay TV companies in the country. I had worked my way up through the ranks, putting myself up for promotions whenever I saw an opportunity to earn more for my family, but I was expected to be on call twenty-four-seven. As the manager of television advertising programs for 60-plus markets, I had hired smart individuals with critical thinking skills to serve on my team, but it was a stressful job. I had two cell phones, and they were always ringing.

"Jeff," my friend said to me when he noticed this, "emergency room surgeons have more vacation and time off than you do!"

I was working 70 hours a week and sleeping three to four hours a night. I was haggard, stressed, and now this. My wife was losing her job.

Could we afford it?

I didn't know.

Fast Fact: *Nearly half of all retirees say they retired earlier than expected.*[4]

WHAT NOBODY IS TELLING YOU

I'm just going to pause things right here because this is the biggest thing that people want to know: *Can we afford to retire?* My wife's story isn't all that unusual. Especially since the pandemic, millions of people found themselves surplussed or experiencing job loss.[5]

It's not so easy to just jump back into the job market after reaching the highpoint of a career. Most people are earning their highest salaries late in life, after years of

---

[4] Retirement Confidence Survey, 2023 Fact Sheet, Expectations about Retirement, EBRI, https://www.ebri.org/retirement/retirement-confidence-survey Accessed 1/05/2024.
[5] Fry, Richard, The Pace Of Boomer Retirements Has Accelerated in The Past Year, Pew Research Center, Nov. 2020, https://www.pewresearch.org/short-reads/2020/11/09/the-pace-of-boomer-retirements-has-accelerated-in-the-past-year/ Accessed 10/12/2023.

accruing credibility and expertise. Not just any job will do. How will you replace this lost income?

There's also the question of saving. If you got a late start in saving for retirement, the U.S. government allows you to make catch-up contributions. This can really turbocharge a nest egg and many people take advantage of this. But what happens if that time gets cut short? How will you replace those lost savings?

Another issue is healthcare. Most group health plans allow you to extend your healthcare coverage after leaving a job, anywhere from 18 to 36 months through COBRA. You must be 65 years old before you can qualify for Medicare. How will you get healthcare benefits *after* your COBRA period ends and *before* Medicare kicks in?

While you might just buy healthcare coverage on the open market, there's still the question of how you'll pay for it. The IRS charges penalties for early withdrawals from retirement accounts. Spending money from a retirement account such as an IRA or 401(k) *before* age 59½ is considered an early distribution. Individuals must pay an *additional* 10 percent penalty tax for early withdrawals—in addition to the taxes already owed—unless an exception applies.[6]

Last but not least, there's the question of how you will make this money last *even longer* than you were planning, now that you're retiring early.

---

[6] IRS, Retirement Topics - Exceptions to Tax on Early Distributions, August 2023, https://www.irs.gov/retirement-plans/plan-participant-employee/retirement-topics-tax-on-early-distributions#:~:text=Generally%2C%20the%20amounts%20an%20individual,tax%20unless%20an%20exception%20applies Accessed 1/09/2024.

Early retirement might sound tempting, but it's a landscape fraught with hidden traps. I know firsthand because I had to navigate this territory myself before I became an adviser. Retirement accounts allow you to invest in the stock market. Your 401(k), 403(b), TSP, IRAs, SEP IRA—whatever account you use—is 100 percent at **risk**. Making the money last is about more than just earning the highest possible rate of return because of this simple fact:

It's not about how much you have set aside; it's about the management of this money.

Has anybody told you this?

As nice as that big pile of money looks, how would you feel watching it shrink by 10 percent? By 25 percent? Let's talk real dollars: how would you feel about losing $250,000 while also making a $50,000 withdraw on this money?

The Great Recession of 2008 was a rude awakening for the many people who hadn't realized that these accounts were susceptible to loss. As I mentioned earlier, if you are in the stock market, nobody can promise that you won't lose this money. So, before you retire, you also have some allocation decisions to make.

Now, there's no need to get nervous about this part. You already know how to do this despite what the brokers on Wall Street might tell you. There's no need for fancy pie charts or colorful graphs or one-size-fits-all questionnaires.

All you need to understand is what got you here.

Fast Fact: *The World Economic Forum reports that most people will live past mandatory retirement age by another 20 to 30 years.*[7]

WHAT YOU DID & WHY IT WORKS

Let's talk about the investment strategy that got you here.

To save for retirement, you put a *portion* of every paycheck into the stock market.

At the same time, you also kept a certain amount of money in the bank, in safe money vehicles. This allowed you to pay your mortgage, your rent, to buy groceries and pay the bills.

You also kept a certain amount of money in a savings account for emergencies and unexpected repairs.

Are you with me so far? One paycheck, three different places: your investments, your income, and your emergency fund.

Did you ever at any point put 100 percent of your paycheck in the stock market?

No! Of course, not—most of us have bills to pay.

So now, here we are at or near retirement. What are people doing with the money they have saved?

They are retiring with 100 percent of their income sitting in the stock market.

Does that sound like a good idea to you? Have you ever employed this strategy before?

---

[7] Nazeri, Haleh, We desperately need to disrupt our approach to retirement saving, World Economic Forum, March 2022, https://www.weforum.org/agenda/2022/03/why-the-concept-of-retirement-needs-to-retire/ Accessed 2/02/2023.

No! Absolutely not. You knew when you were saving the money that you had bills to pay. Now, here you are no longer working, and you still have bills to pay. So, let me ask you:

How will you pay those bills if 100 percent of your money is sitting at risk in the stock market?

This isn't a rhetorical question—really think about this. If you suddenly lost 25 percent of your paycheck tomorrow, how would that change the way you live? Would you have to sell your house? Your car? Get a second job?

Losing money in the stock market can result in the same thing. If you lose income money in retirement, that's like taking a 25 percent reduction to your salary. If this isn't what you envisioned for yourself in retirement, keep reading, because this book is going to show you how to think like an adviser to design a solution.

Fast Fact: *During the financial crisis that triggered the Great Recession, the S&P 500 index lost 53% of its value from October 2007 to February 2009.*[8]

WHAT YOU NEED TO DO NOW

You may have done everything right when saving for retirement, but what you do next is even more important. The way you manage your savings during your last few years of your working life is critical.

---

[8] Parker, Kim, and Fry, Richard, More than half of U.S. households have some investment in the stock market, Pew Research Center March 2020 https://www.pewresearch.org/fact-tank/2020/03/25/more-than-half-of-u-s-households-have-some-investment-in-the-stock-market/ Accessed 1/20/2023.

Smart investors learn how to *preserve* their savings in safe money vehicles *before* they retire. This will ensure that a sudden downturn in the market will not affect your retirement timeline.

The 2008 stock market crash forced many individuals to postpone their retirement plans, as the financial downturn eroded their nest eggs just years before they intended to leave the workforce. In my experience, it took the average investor 12 years to recover from this loss. Earning the money back is never as easy as most people are led to believe. The reason has to do with the mathematical reality of **account value restoration**.

It goes like this:

Imagine you invest $100 in a mutual fund. Soon after, your phone buzzes with an alert notifying you that the fund has dropped by 10 percent. You check your account and confirm it's now worth $90. A 10 percent decrease led to a $10 loss. After some time, however, you receive another alert, this time saying that the fund has gained 10 percent. *Hooray*, you think. Naturally, you're eager to check your balance, expecting to have fully recovered from your loss.

The fund dipped by 10 percent but then climbed 10 percent, so now, your account should be made whole, right?

Yet, when you check, your account value shows only $99.

That's when it dawns on you: a 10 percent gain on a $90 account is just $9, not the $10 you initially lost. To truly break even, you'd actually need a gain of slightly more than 11 percent.

Now, imagine adding multiple zeros to that initial investment amount, and factor in the added challenge of withdrawing an income from an ever-changing account. What are the odds you'll ever break even?

The math gets worse the bigger the loss. Experience a loss of 20 percent, and you'd require a 25 percent gain to get back to your original balance. A 30 percent loss would necessitate nearly a 42 percent gain just to break even. And if your losses totaled 50 percent, you would need a whopping 100 percent gain to restore your account.

Check out the visual below using quarters to simplify things.

Source: Magellan Financial. Not indicative of investment performance.

To solve the income problem created by this distressing math requires that you shift your mindset. As you approach retirement, you'll want to transition *out* of accumulation mode and *into* preservation mode. Once you do retire, you will need to shift your thinking again to a distribution mentality. This is why this book is titled *Safe Money Mindset*.

A *Safe Money Mindset* is a mash-up of how you think about investing, how you plan to spend your wealth, and how you will derive future income. This mindset is a unique approach to building a retirement portfolio that is on all fronts stable, inflation resilient, and able to support a lifestyle you won't outlive.

The first step to achieving this *Safe Money Mindset* is understanding the financial phase that you are currently in.

Fast Fact: *Running out of money is the top fear in retirement.*[9]

YOUR 3 FINANCIAL PHASES

Every investor passes through three distinct financial phases. Those phases are the **accumulation phase,** the **preservation phase** and the **distribution phase**.

During your working years, you accumulate and grow your assets. In the business of financial planning, we call this your *accumulation phase*. We just discussed how most people, if they are disciplined, can achieve some nice growth during this phase.

---

[9] O'Brien, Elizabeth, Running Out of Money Is the Top Retirement Worry: Report, Barrons, June 2023, https://www.barrons.com/articles/money-top-retirement-worry-2830cc9f Accessed 8/15/2023.

This financial phase benefits from long-term *passive investment strategies* such as a **buy-and-hold strategy** and **dollar-cost averaging**. The reason these passive strategies work is because you aren't spending the money. Basically, if you keep putting away the money, over time the money continues to grow. Whether the stock market goes up, down, or sideways, as long as you don't touch this money, your account should move upward, which is exactly the outcome you want.

Once you start to think about how you will spend this money for income, everything changes. Your mind will start to slowly shift from a *growth* focus to an *income* focus. That can sometimes take years. The sooner you shift that focus, the more secure your retirement income will be.

If you can make the shift early like I did, anywhere from five to 10 years out from your own retirement, then you will be entering the preservation phase. In this phase, your mindset should be on the *preservation* of what you have grown. During this phase, we look at portioning off some of the money required for your income into a safe money strategy to better protect this money from market **volatility**.

During retirement, investors enter their *distribution phase*. This phase begins when you're no longer putting money into your portfolio or retirement accounts; instead, *you're taking the money out*.

For some people, the fear of running out might prompt them to stay in the market to keep earning those high returns, but as we discussed, you already know that keeping 100 percent of your income in the stock market isn't a good idea. However, given today's longer retirement, with inflation and the likelihood of a long-term care event, most people can't afford to get out of the market altogether. They require some combination of short-term and long-term investing strategies and income planning tools that employ low to moderate risk.

This is where the *Three Worlds of Money* comes in to help you design a customized strategy.

The following visual gives you an idea of what age you might enter each of these three phases. As you can see, the wide age ranges indicate the need for financial advice tailored to your timeline and not someone else's.

Your Three Financial Phases

A - Accumulation
20s, 30s, 40s, 50s, 60s

P - Preservation
40s, 50s, 60s, 70s

D - Distribution
60s, 70s, 80s, 90+

Source: Magellan Financial

To be successful during the preservation and distribution phases requires much more finesse and forethought than the strategies used during the accumulation phase. It only makes sense when you think about it: retirement for most of us is going to last a long time. We all saw how much inflation increased the cost of things after the pandemic, and we know that the cost of healthcare has historically been the highest-inflated product on the market.[10] These are the reasons why I searched long and hard for a **fiduciary** adviser who specialized in comprehensive financial planning rather than just wealth building and portfolio management.

You might also want to inquire about the adviser's firm and the scope of its services. Can they give you access to a tax specialist? An attorney? Do they have a Medicare specialist on staff? Are they able to run a Social Security optimization report to help you get a filing strategy?

In short, can your adviser get you the access you need to investments, strategies, and solutions specific to the financial phase you're in?

Fast Fact: *Only 23% of Americans have a comprehensive written plan for retirement.*[11]

---

[10] Wager, Emma, et al, How does medical inflation compare to inflation in the rest of the economy? KFF, Nov 2022, https://www.kff.org/health-costs/issue-brief/how-does-medical-inflation-compare-to-inflation-in-the-rest-of-the-economy/ Accessed 3/8/2023.
[11] Deaton, Holly, Most Americans Have No Financial Plan. The Ones Who Do Praise the Benefits, RIA Intel, May 2022, https://www.riaintel.com/article/2aucrzsa72lr93ymbe7eo/wealth-management/most-americans-have-no-financial-plan-the-ones-who-do-praise-the-benefits Accessed 2/21/2023.

A TAKE-ACTION KIND OF GUY

I'll never forget the first time I heard about the *Three Worlds of Money* concept. It was my good friend Joan who referred me to the financial advisers at Quest. She had worked with Gene Wittstock and his money manager Bill.

"Set up a meeting with them," she told me. "They will be able to tell you whether or not you can afford early retirement."

We had the meeting. Gene talked to us like human beings. He listened first and asked questions about who we were—our jobs, hobbies, and the ages of our children. Then, he explained the *Three Worlds of Money* concept. We gave him our info and financials and scheduled a second appointment for one week later.

When we arrived for that second appointment, Gene started going through the *Three Worlds of Money* concept again.

"Excuse me, Gene," I interrupted him. "You already explained all this to us last time."

"Oh, I know," Gene said. "But you gotta see this two or three times before it starts to sink in."

"Oh no," I said. "I already got it. This is exactly what I've been looking for."

Gene looked at me skeptically.

"It's true," my wife Medina spoke up for me. "He explained it all to me on the ride here this morning."

"Okay," Gene said. "Why don't you teach it to me."

Feeling a little sheepish, I got up and went through it all. His jaw dropped.

"Okay," he said, "so, you're a fast learner. We'll just go forward, and I'll tell you how it is."

Gene went up to the white board and wrote out some numbers. These were our numbers. Then he talked to both of us.

"According to the math, yes, you can afford for your wife to take the deal and retire early—but only because of Jeff's job. Jeff, you must keep earning this much money or more, and you must keep putting those contributions into your retirement account. If you don't, the two of you will run out of money."

We left that meeting with a clear idea of where we stood.

The following week, we met for a third time to go over all the paperwork and set the plan in motion. During this meeting, I told Gene a story about how stressed and overworked I was at my current job.

"I went to see a movie this weekend with my family," I explained. "My phone went off three times during the film. Later, when I called my boss back, she yelled at me for taking two hours to return her call. So, I asked her, 'What are your expectations as to my availability to you?' And she replied, 'Twenty-four seven.' I told her, 'That's unrealistic! I'm not going to sleep with my phone on my pillow. We're not curing cancer here—this is television! Why put so much pressure on commercials?'"

Gene listened to my story and all but offered me a job.

"Man," he said, "wouldn't it be great if you could leave your current position and come here to work with us? I've never seen somebody pick up on this stuff so quickly."

I went home that day with a big smile on my face. It was nice of Gene to pay me such a compliment. My wife and I had gotten our retirement planning done. We'd shifted into a *preservation phase* with our money. Two weeks later, Medina stopped working. I continued at my current job, and for a while everything was good.

Then, my boss's boss got replaced. From day one, he did *not* like me. This added to my already significant stress load. I wasn't getting along with my current boss, either, when I got wind of a plot they had to restructure things. Once that happened, I realized, my current position would no longer exist.

I knew my chances of surviving this were not good. I also knew that our retirement plan was dependent on me earning.

I called up a friend in human resources.

"After they restructure things," I explained, "my current job won't exist. So, what happens if I don't apply for another job within the company?"

"I would have to write you up a severance package," she said. "You would get one year of salary—they would basically pay you to leave."

My next call was to my wife, Medina.

"Things are not going to end well for me here," I said, explaining everything.

"What are you going to do?" she asked.

"I think I'm going to give Gene a call."

"Oh, honey," she said. "He was just being nice!"

"Maybe," I said. "But I want to do what he does."

I called up Gene. I knew it was pie in the sky, but I had to try. I explained that I could come and work for his firm for one year for a minimal salary while I studied, got my license, and learned the trade. I was betting on myself more than anything because, given what I had just been through, I knew I was passionate about the subject of retirement planning.

Gene listened, prayed about it, and called me back two days later.

"Everything is pointing to yes," he said. "Let's do this."

I talked it over with Medina and put in my two weeks' notice.

Two years later, I was telling this story during dinner seminars while teaching retirement planning workshops. I believe in this system of planning *so much*, I left my job and came here to help teach other people how to do it.

Yes, I'm a *take action* kind of guy. So, I'm going to ask you to do the same. At the end of each chapter, I will propose a few action steps you can take now to embrace the safe money mindset and apply it to your current situation today.

CHANGE YOUR MINDSET: NEXT STEPS

EVALUATE WHERE YOU'RE CURRENTLY AT.

- What financial phase are you currently in?
- Do your investments match your current risk tolerance?
- What percent of your portfolio would you be comfortable with losing?
- What percentage of your portfolio would you like to shift into a safe money strategy?
- What one step can you take right now, today, to help you get to where you want to be? (Hint: read the next chapter.)

STEP 2

IDENTIFY YOUR 5 BIGGEST THREATS

"Whether you think you can, or you think you can't —you're right."

~ Henry Ford

Let me tell you a story about one of the first clients I ever met with. Due to health reasons, Sabrina had to take an early retirement. This was a situation I knew all too well. When she retired at the age of 56, she met with her broker, and then promptly lost a substantial amount of her retirement savings. This loss wasn't from the stock market—it was due to the IRS penalties for early withdrawals.

Sabrina was understandably puzzled. She had done everything her broker told her to do. She'd saved, invested, and then retired. She had to use this money for income—that was why she had saved it! But now, because she wasn't yet age 59½, every time she spent it, there would be a 10 percent penalty on top of the taxes she already owed.

Maddening!

This was not what she had envisioned spending her money on.

A year went by. Through a friend, Sabrina learned that the advisers over at Quest had experience avoiding these early withdrawal penalties. She felt a surge of hope and scheduled a meeting with us.

Unfortunately, by the time we met with her, it was too late to reverse the penalty.[12]

Stories like this make me angry.

Every day I see people who did everything right when they *saved* the money, only to be misguided when it came time to *spend* the money. Had Sabrina consulted with us initially, before she'd done anything with the money, we could have advised her differently. We would have asked that she retain a significant portion of her assets in the original 401(k). Why?

There is a little-known IRS provision referred to as the *Rule of 55* that allows for penalty-free withdrawals.

This rule allows for penalty-free withdrawals from a 401(k) if the account holder is 55 or older at the time they leave their employer—whether they were laid off, fired, or quit. You have to follow the guidelines, and, of course, the distributions are not tax-free—you still owe income taxes on the money. But had Sabrina utilized this rule, she would have literally saved thousands of dollars because she could have bypassed the 10 percent penalty.

---

[12] Based on a true story. Names and details have been changed to protect the individual's privacy. Your own results may vary.

Unfortunately, the rules dictate that you can only withdraw funds from your most recent 401(k) or 403(b) account for the exception to apply. Sabrina's broker had rolled over her *entire* 401(k) into an IRA, so now, that option was off the table. Had he even left just a *little* money in the original 401(k) account, that would have helped her, and we could have applied the *Rule of 55*. Instead, she was left saddled with the 10 percent penalty.

Why would her broker do this to her? Why hadn't he informed her of this rule?

The most likely explanations are either a lack of awareness or—and I hate to think this, but I've seen it all too often—a deliberate act of greed. By rolling over the entire 401(k) into an IRA, the broker was able to boost his management fees by consolidating all her assets into one managed account.

Do you see why this makes me so upset? I wanted to go drive down the street and talk to this broker. I wanted to ask him, "What are you doing??!! Is it greed? Ignorance? Either way, you should not be in the business!!!"

I am happy to say that we were able to help Sabrina save some money by utilizing something called a 72T option. This allowed her to receive a portion of her income penalty-free from the IRS, but it was far from ideal. She still had to seek part-time employment to earn what the 72T couldn't get her because, until she reached age 59½, she would continue to pay that 10 percent penalty.

This is the exact kind of thing I ran into when I was trying to figure out an early retirement for my wife. We encountered the same issues at the other brokerage firms because Medina also owed taxes on the buyout money—and it was a huge tax bill, not even counting the 10 percent penalty! When we brought this to her tax person, he chalked it up to a "lack of withholding," but that didn't sound right. I knew it wasn't the full story and now I know why.

There are ways to manage tax-deferred accounts—smart, little-known strategies that can help you avoid paying thousands in taxes and taking a hit. There are many ways a person can lose money in retirement. True planning looks at *all* the issues: taxes, inflation, and market risk. It looks at what can happen to your income if you lose a spouse. It asks uncomfortable questions about the subject of long-term care. The fiduciary adviser does this because that's the job: to put the best interests of the client above his own.

This is what everybody needs to understand:

Unless your plan considers all five of these areas, you stand to lose during the years ahead.

Market risk is a concern, yes, but it isn't even close to the only risk that retirees face today. There are a lot more threats to consider and gaining protection from them is not as simple as a one-size-fits-all solution. Let's take a look at each of these areas and talk about actionable steps.

Fast Fact: *Americans hold $6.3 trillion in untaxed wealth inside their 401(k) plans.*[13]

---

[13] Investment Company Institute, 401(k) Resource Center, ICI Global, September 2022, https://www.ici.org/401k Accessed 1/04/2024.

RISK #1: TAXES

During your working years, you're told not to worry about taxes in retirement. You've probably heard countless financial gurus preach the mantra: "Always tax-defer your retirement contributions because your earning years are your highest tax years." Well, I'm here to shed light on a different perspective. I've worked with countless individuals in their 70s, 80s, and even 90s who are currently shouldering a higher tax burden than they ever faced during their working years.

This can happen if you save in a retirement account such as an IRA or 401(k) without giving any thought to future taxes.

I admit, the deal starts out as a pretty good one. The money comes out of your paycheck *before* this income is taxed, it goes into your retirement account where it grows *without* being tax, and it continues to grow *without being taxed*, compounding interest. This allows you to accumulate a nice big pot of money.

Now, the closer you get to the time of retirement, the bigger that pot of money grows. For most people, their IRA or 401(k) is the single largest monetary account they own. You might also have a 403(b), 457, or a Thrift Savings Plan (TSP), but those are just other examples. The majority of people who save for retirement do so in tax-deferred accounts.

The problem? **You haven't paid any taxes on this money.** Not on the amount you initially put in, and not on the growth.

Unless this money sits inside a **Roth IRA**, *you still owe income tax on every penny of what you have saved.* That means Uncle Sam gets a certain percentage of every dollar you take out.

But wait—he also has rules about how much money you must take out and when. If someone tax defers a lot of money and doesn't pay taxes on it fast enough in retirement, then the IRS will *force* withdrawals, which can raise your income tax level starting in your mid-70s. Failing to follow these rules will cost you even more money in penalties. Whenever you go to spend this money, you never know what unintended side effects might be triggered.

Withdrawals from these accounts can increase your income, your marginal tax rate, the amount of tax you pay on your Social Security income, and the amount you pay in Medicare premiums.

During your retirement, tax rates will also increase and decrease with different lawmakers in office. We have no control over what Washington does with the tax rates and none of us know for a fact what will happen with taxes over time.

At the same time, as the Baby Boomers retire, the number of people drawing on federal entitlement programs like Social Security and Medicare is rising significantly. There are several ways the federal government can try to continue funding these programs. They can decrease or restructure benefits for retirees, they can borrow the money, or *they can raise taxes.*

While you have zero control over tax law and what Congress does, you do have 100 percent control over what you do with this money now. That is the difference between *planning for* vs. *paying* your taxes, and we will be talking more about this in Step Five.

Fast Fact: *Unlucky investors who experienced a poor sequence of returns are 31% more likely to run out of money.*[14]

RISK #2: MARKET RISK

Systematic **risk**, or market risk in the stock market, is unpredictable and impossible to completely avoid, regardless of the amount of diversification. The only way to mitigate its bite is by investing in assets that have no **correlation**. We will be talking more about asset allocation in Step Three.

Examples of market risk include:
- **Recessions**: a recession can cause a decline in various asset classes simultaneously.
- **Interest rate fluctuations**: when interest rates rise, the value of bonds generally falls, affecting bond heavy portfolios. Higher borrowing costs can negatively affect corporate profitability, affecting stock prices. Higher interest rates dampen the housing market which

---

[14] Khang, Kevin I., and Clarke, Andrew S., Safeguarding Retirement in a Bear Market, Vanguard, June 2020, page 1, https://www.vanguard.co.uk/content/dam/intl/europe/documents/en/whitepapers/safeguarding-retirement-bear-market.pdf Accessed 12/29/2023.

also affects related industries like construction and home improvement.
- **Political events**: government decisions, like regulatory changes or changes in tax law, can dramatically impact industries. Also, tariffs and trade wars can affect international companies and commodity prices can increase.
- **Global events**: large scale events have the capacity to affect markets worldwide. Wars, for example, can cause significant market volatility. Also, global pandemics can disrupt supply chains and slow consumer spending, impacting virtually all sectors. Large scale natural disasters can also affect global markets if they disrupt key industries or resources.

Market risk is the risk of losing **principal** and interest due to a market correction. If that correction happens sometime during the years just before or after retirement, you might not have time to make up for those losses. We talked earlier about the reality of account value restoration. That could seriously compromise your portfolio's ability to generate income, causing you to outlive your savings.

Now, I'm going to unveil another phenomenon that you have no control over, known as **sequence risk**.

The *sequence of returns* is the order that you receive a gain or a loss. This is something that you have absolutely no control over, and yet, if you experience a poor sequence of returns just before or after you retire, you stand a much greater chance of *running out of money*. This is known in the industry as *sequence risk*.

Let me share an example.

Two people can retire with *the exact same amount of money,* average *the exact same returns,* and withdraw *the exact same income.* And yet—one of them will be in danger of running out of money while the other one does just fine.

Why?

Sequence risk.

This risk is especially important for people who are at or near retirement to consider. If you are unlucky enough to retire just before a major market downturn, and you are withdrawing from your investments for income, then you may never recover from the double loss, even if the markets improve. This is why it's important to diversify into non-correlated assets.

Take a look at the charts shown on the following pages. The returns each investor receives are the same but with the order, or sequence of returns, reversed.

INVESTOR A

Account balance after 20 years: $304,680

Assuming $50K Annual Withdrawal (Average Return 6.91%)

SP 500 YEAR 2001 -2020

Year	Beg. Of Year Acct. Value	End Of Year Acct. Value	Earnings Rate
2001	$1,000,000	$819,570	-13.1%
2002	$819,570	$578,070	-23.37%
2003	$578,070	$680,570	26.38%
2004	$680,570	$691,780	8.99%
2005	$691,780	$662,540	3.00%
2006	$662,540	$702,770	13.62%
2007	$702,770	$677,580	3.53%
2008	$677,580	$366,810	-38.49%
2009	$366,810	$402,840	23.45%
2010	$402,840	$404,330	12.78%
2011	$404,330	$354,320	0.00%
2012	$354,320	$351,820	13.41%
2013	$351,820	$405,960	29.60%
2014	$405,960	$402,200	11.39%
2015	$402,200	$349,280	-0.73%
2016	$349,280	$332,580	9.54%
2017	$332,580	$347,170	19.42%
2018	$347,170	$275,510	-6.24%
2019	$275,510	$305,080	28.88%
2020	$305,080	$304,680	16.26%

Source: Magellan Financial. For illustrative purposes only based on the S&P 500 Index from the years 2001 to 2020. The results presented above do not represent any actual investment performance or the actual account of our investors.

INVESTOR B

Account balance after 20 years: $1,619,100

Assuming $50K Annual Withdrawal (Average Return 6.91%)

SP 500 YEAR 2020 -2001

Year	Beg. Of Year Acct. Value	End Of Year Acct. Value	Earnings Rate
2020	$1,000,000	$1,112,590	16.26%
2019	$1,112,590	$1,383,880	28.88%
2018	$1,383,880	$1,247,570	-6.24%
2017	$1,247,570	$1,439,984	19.42%
2016	$1,439,984	$1,527,130	9.54%
2015	$1,527,130	$1,466,040	-0.73%
2014	$1,466,040	$1,583,030	11.39%
2013	$1,583,030	$2,001,620	29.60%
2012	$2,001,620	$2,219,960	13.41%
2011	$2,219,960	$2,169,890	0.00%
2010	$2,169,890	$2,397,260	12.78%
2009	$2,397,260	$2,909,510	23.45%
2008	$2,909,510	$1,739,760	-38.49%
2007	$1,739,760	$1,751,170	3.53%
2006	$1,751,170	$1,939,670	13.62%
2005	$1,939,670	$1,947,880	3.00%
2004	$1,947,880	$2,073,060	8.99%
2003	$2,073,306	$2,569,940	26.38%
2002	$2,569,940	$1,919,450	-23.37%
2001	$1,919,450	$1,619,100	-13.1%

Source: Magellan Financial. For illustrative purposes only based on the S&P 500 Index from the years 2001 to 2020. The results presented above do not represent any actual investment performance or the actual account of our investors.

Both investors started with the same amount of money; both averaged a 6.91 percent return; both withdrew $50,000 a year for income. But Investor A received his losses early on, and as a result, his $1 million portfolio dwindled to only $304,680.

Meanwhile, Investor B experienced those exact same negative returns, just later in retirement, while taking the same withdrawals, and this investor has a portfolio balance of over $1.5 million.

Obviously, no one wants to be the unlucky investor, but as I mentioned earlier, you have no control over what the sequence of returns will be in the years just after you retire. The only thing you *can* be proactive about is how to safeguard and protect this money.

Fast Fact: *More than 70% of individuals aged 50 and older are concerned that inflation will cause serious economic hardship during their retirement.*[15]

RISK #3: INFLATION

Discussing inflation is essential because it erodes the real value of retirement savings and fixed income streams, such as pensions or annuities. A gallon of milk today will not cost the same as a gallon of milk tomorrow. Over the 12 months ending in June 2022, the Consumer Price Index for American consumers increased 9.1 percent, the largest

---

[15] Block, Sandra, Protect Your Retirement Income from Inflation, Kiplinger, September 2022 https://www.kiplinger.com/personal-finance/inflation/605175/protect-your-retirement-income-from-inflation Accessed 1/24/2023.

12-month increase since the 12-month period ending November 1981.[16] Energy prices rose by 41.6 percent; food at home rose 12.2 percent. The price of gas? That saw a 60.2 percent increase over this same time span.[17]

The year 2013 marked the 100th anniversary of the consumer price index—the index that measures the change in prices. To commemorate the anniversary, the Bureau of Labor Statistics revealed its cumulative data in the following chart to give you an idea of inflation's curve over a 30-year period. The line on the top represents the increase in medical care.

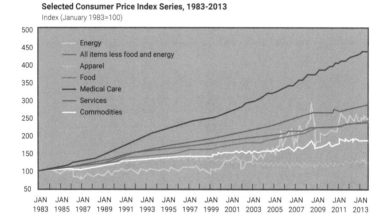

Source: U.S. Bureau of Labor Statistics.

Even when inflation rates are low, the effect is felt more by retirees, many of whom live on a fixed income. Therefore, it's not just important that you are growing your

---

[16] U.S. Bureau of Labor Statistics, TED: The Economics Daily, July 2022, https://www.bls.gov/opub/ted/2022/consumer-prices-up-9-1-percent-over-the-year-ended-june-2022-largest-increase-in-40-years.htm#:~:text=Bureau%20of%20Labor%20Statistics%2C%20U.S.,.htm%20(visited%20January%2016%2C Accessed 1/16/2024.
[17] Ibid.

money every year during retirement; **you also want to grow your income**.

While emphasizing the importance of *safe money vehicles*, it's also critical to acknowledge that some growth assets may still be necessary to counteract inflation's impact. This is why we must utilize the *Three Worlds of Money*. We can't just rely on the protection and hybrid buckets. We must also utilize the potential for growth in order to stay ahead of inflation. You will be meeting those *Three Worlds of Money* in our next chapter.

Fast Fact: *A significant share of older Americans underestimate how long they are going to live.*[18]

RISK #4: LONG-TERM CARE OR FUTURE HEALTHCARE

In crafting a secure retirement plan, it's imperative to account for the unpredictability of long-term care and future healthcare expenses. Such costs can quickly undermine a meticulously balanced portfolio. Therefore, it's essential to explore a range of financial tools, such as long-term care insurance, health savings accounts, and annuities designed for healthcare costs, to bolster your financial defenses.

Consider establishing a specialized emergency fund dedicated solely to healthcare, distinct from a general

---

[18] De Visè, Daniel, Retirees are underestimating how long they will live, The Hill, July 2023, https://thehill.com/business/4076702-retirees-are-underestimating-how-long-they-will-live/ Accessed 1/08/2024.

emergency fund, as an additional safeguard. Be aware of the limitations of government programs like Medicare and Medicaid. Evaluate asset-protection strategies, like adding a certain type of **trust**, to enhance your financial security. A truly comprehensive retirement strategy must incorporate planning for healthcare and long-term care expenses; neglecting this aspect can jeopardize even the safest of financial plans.

Why do I emphasize this risk? It's long been reported that more than half of all 65-year-olds will require some form of long-term care (LTC), but LTC is often misunderstood. Long-term care refers to a wide range of services that you might need as your body ages, and these services could be performed at an assisted living center or in the comfort of your own home. Services range from simple custodial duties such as meal preparation or taking out the garbage to more intrinsic nursing services or 24-hour care.

- 48 percent of people turning age 65 will need some form of paid LTC services during their lifetime.[19]
- 24 percent of people turning 65 will require paid LTC for *more than two years.*[20]
- 15 percent of people turning age 65 will spend more than 2 years in a nursing home.[21]
- Men will need LTC for an average of 2.2 years.[22]

---

[19] Benz, Christine, 100 Must-Know Statistics About Long-Term Care: 2023 Edition, Morningstar, March 2023, https://www.morningstar.com/personal-finance/100-must-know-statistics-about-long-term-care-2023-edition Accessed 7/25/2023.
[20] Ibid.
[21] Ibid.
[22] Ibid.

- Women will need LTC for an average of 3.7 years.[23]
- The 2021 national average for the cost of a private room in a nursing home is $108,405 annually.[24]

Over the last 17 years, Genworth has seen a continuous national increase in the cost of care according to their surveys, and the recent year was no exception. Paying for these expenses is not only unpleasant to think about, but also a complicated problem to solve. Insurance companies have been rapidly exiting the long-term care market because of rising claims, low mortality rates, and higher prices in coverage than what most people can afford.[25] At the same time, innovative solutions are being offered using other policy options.

Because you know your health history better than anyone, this is an area where your advisor must customize a solution for you.

Fast Fact: *One out of every 3 seniors die from Alzheimer's or dementia, and in 2023 it cost the nation $345 billion.*[26]

---

[23] Ibid.
[24] Genworth, Key Cost of Care Findings, 2021, page 1, https://www.genworth.com/aging-and-you/finances/cost-of-care.html Accessed 1/23/2023.
[25] Warshawsky, Mark J., The Second Failed Attempt at Public Insurance For Long-Term Services And Supports, Health Affairs, February 2022. https://www.healthaffairs.org/do/10.1377/forefront.20220131.939312/ Accessed 1/23/2023.
[26] Alzheimer's Association, Facts, and Figures, 2023 https://www.alz.org/alzheimers-dementia/facts-figures Accessed 3/29/2023.

RISK #5: DEATH OF A SPOUSE

The loss of a spouse is an emotionally devastating event that carries with it significant financial implications as well. When your spouse passes away, you will automatically lose at minimum one source of guaranteed lifetime income in the form of Social Security. You might also lose pension income unless that person did some planning. Losing these guaranteed checks creates a huge loss of income that somehow needs to be made up.

Another critical point to remember is that a **Required Minimum Distribution** (RMD) from retirement accounts will remain unchanged, despite a change in marital status. This can result in higher taxes for the surviving spouse, who now files as a single taxpayer. Not only will they be receiving less income, but their tax rate could increase by up to 83 percent.[27]

Most people in this situation find that the cost to maintain their lifestyle stays relatively the same, yet studies find that widows experience an income reduction of 35 to 40 percent upon their spouse's death[28].

---

[27] Statement based on the mathematical calculations of a 10% increase from a base rate of 12%. The portion taxed at 22% will pay a rate that is 83% higher than the portion taxed at 12%.

[28] Every CRS Report. "Congressional Research Service report: Social Security and Vulnerable Groups—Policy Options to Aid Widows." January 2020, R46182 CRS Report, https://www.everycrsreport.com/reports/R46182.html Accessed 1/23/2023.

Even if you receive a 35 percent pay cut, as a single taxpayer, you could still find yourself paying higher taxes. Take a look at the visual below.

WHAT WILL YOUR NEW TAX RATE BE?

TAX RATE	FOR SINGLE FILERS	MARRIED FILING JOINTLY
10%	$0 - $11,600	$0 - $23,200
12%	$11,600 - $47,150	$23,200 - $94,300
22%	$47,150 - $100,525	$94,300 - $201,050
24%	$100,525 - $191,950	$201,050 - $383,900
32%	$191,950 - $243,725	$383,900 - $487,450
35%	$243,725 - $609,350	$487,450 - $731,200
37%	$609,350 or more	$731,200 or more

83% INCREASE (between 12% and 22% brackets)

Source: Magellan Financial using IRS 2024 tax brackets.[29]

To mitigate this, consider strategies like Roth IRA conversions or strategic account drawdowns well in advance. Additionally, be prepared for potential reductions in Social Security and pension income. If you are married, advanced planning with stable income sources like life insurance or annuities is essential. Grieving is already hard and money problems are stressful. In essence, proactive financial planning can alleviate some of the financial burdens that come with the loss of a spouse, allowing for a smoother emotional and financial transition.

---

[29] Statement of increase based on the mathematical calculations of a 10% increase from a base rate of 12%. The portion taxed at 22% will pay a rate that is 83% higher than the portion taxed at 12%.

Fast Fact: *There is a persistent financial literacy gap with a much higher percentage of women displaying low investor knowledge as compared to men.*[30]

WHAT 20-YEAR PERIOD ARE YOU RETIRING IN?

I was early into my career in advertising when my wife and I experienced the recession of 2008. Our 401(k)s got hit by 30 percent, and I didn't like it one bit, but my personal situation was nothing compared to all the other people who were hurting. I was in my *accumulation phase*, still working and drawing on a paycheck.

I told my wife, "We're going to tighten our belts and max out our contributions because stocks right now are trading low."

I recognized the recession as an opportunity to make a lot of money. Ford Motor Company stocks were trading at that time for $1—so cheap! We lived on a budget, maxed out our retirement accounts, and invested every dollar we could.

Meanwhile, I saw what happened to my co-workers in their 60s who took the same hit. They had done nothing to preserve their savings, and so now this loss extended how long they would have to keep working by several more years. That was when my eyes were opened to the significance of the investor's timeline.

---

[30] Subran, Ludovic, et al, Playing with a squared ball: the financial literacy gender gap, Allianz Research, July 2023, Accessed 1/08/2024.

Now, when I sit down to talk with someone about their retirement plan, I ask them to think of it this way: *What 20-year period are you going to be retiring in?*

Remember the charts earlier that highlighted sequence risk? Grab any 20-year period of history, and you'll see a huge difference as to what can happen depending on the year you retire. Systematic risk can hit everything, even real estate, which is often considered an uncorrelated asset. That's what happened in 2008, and it happened again during the pandemic, only with a twist. When people weren't able to pay rent due to layoffs and shutdowns, landlords weren't receiving any rental income, and legally, they weren't allowed to evict anyone.[31]

Dividend income also took a beating in 2020, when nearly 190 U.S.-listed companies *stopped paying dividends*, and, two years later, 38.5 percent of them had yet to reinstate dividends—and we're talking about big companies like Boeing and Walt Disney.[32]

Could you go two years without an income?

One myth perpetuated by the world of finance is that "the market always comes back." That might be true, but will it come back during the timeline that you need it to?

When you're early in your accumulation years, you have time to make the money back. My own 401(k) recovered within one year because I was saving aggressively and

---

[31] Federal Register, Temporary Halt in Residential Evictions To Prevent the Further Spread of COVID-19, September 2020, https://www.federalregister.gov/documents/2020/09/04/2020-19654/temporary-halt-in-residential-evictions-to-prevent-the-further-spread-of-covid-19 Accessed 12/17/2023.
[32] Maurer, Mark, Some Companies Haven't Paid a Dividend Since 2020. They Might Bring It Back as a Slowdown Looms, Walls Street Journal, August 2022, https://www.wsj.com/articles/some-companies-havent-paid-a-dividend-since-2020-they-might-bring-it-back-as-a-slowdown-looms-11661765401 Accessed 12/26/2023.

buying low. I could afford to do this because both my wife and I were working at the time. When I did the math, I calculated that, had I done nothing different and kept things the same using dollar-cost averaging, it would have taken us seven to eight years to recover our accounts.

Once you enter the *preservation phase*, or are at or near retirement, you don't have years and years to wait for the market to recover, so coming back is a difficult thing. Your best bet with your retirement income is *to not take the risk at all*. We will be looking at the types of programs designed to sustain income levels during recessions and economic downturns in our vehicles chapter, Step Four.

As we close this chapter, I invite you to take the next crucial step in securing your financial future. Whether you find yourself in the *preservation* or *distribution phase* of your financial journey, or you have specific concerns about taxes, risk management, Medicare, or income planning, we're here to help. As a reader of this book, I'd like to offer you a complimentary consultation where we conduct a comprehensive retirement analysis tailored to your unique situation. This consultation is an invaluable opportunity to address your risk concerns and create a roadmap that aligns with your goals. If this sounds appealing to you, reach out to the number below.

If you already have an adviser, that's great, but why not get a second opinion? My neighbor was looking for someone to mow his lawn, and he talked with two or three different people before he found the right guy. And he was just looking for the right person to cut his grass! Why not talk to a couple of advisers, given how important it is to get this right? Find out who can go a bit deeper into the areas that you have questions about.

Whether it's tax law, **estate planning**, or Medicare, don't sell yourself short. One adviser alone can never be the end-all-be-all. Lawyers have a team. Doctors have a team. Why should we expect one person in finance to understand all the elements that will impact a person's fiscal health during a 30-year retirement? Medicare, Medicaid, taxes, Social Security, investments, estate planning, long-term care—how can one person be an expert in all that? There are not enough hours in the day.

At Quest Commonwealth, we employ a team of individuals—lawyers, CPAs, investment advisers, and Medicare specialists—all of whom are held to the fiduciary standard and hand-picked by our CEO, Gene Wittstock. We look forward to partnering with you to ensure that your retirement years are not only secure but also fulfilling. Don't leave your financial future to chance—contact us today to schedule your complimentary consultation and get a second opinion.

CHANGE YOUR MINDSET: NEXT STEPS
GET A SECOND OPINION.

- Contact us for a complimentary, no-obligation second opinion at 1-866-QUEST-01.
- For Michigan residents, call 248-599-1000.
- Visit us at 30700 Telegraph Rd, Ste 1475, Bingham Farms, MI, 48025.

STEP 3

UTILIZE THE THREE WORLDS OF MONEY:
PROTECTION, POTENTIAL, & HYBRID

"Wisdom is knowing what to do next.
Skill is knowing how to do it.
Virtue is doing it."

~ Thomas Jefferson

I was 28 years old when I first met the woman who would become my wife. She was finalizing her divorce and receiving full custody of her daughter. That weekend, Medina's sister dragged her to a Halloween party at her neighbor's house. Medina didn't want to go, but the two of them made costumes—Medina dressing as a sixties flower child.

I had just served 10 years in the Navy and was considering either reenlisting as a reservist or getting out. I wanted a home life and a family. I was living with my sister when she dragged me out to the same Halloween party for her son's best friend.

"I can't go to this," I told her. "I don't even have a costume!"

"I can fix that." My sister grabbed one of those *Scream* masks, pushed it into my hands, and said, "Meet me there."

I arrive wearing the *Scream* mask. I walked into the house, and my sister was the first person I see.

"Hey," she said, "I want to take you over to meet my friend."

She drags me through the room of costumes, brings me over to a group of people, and says, "Anybody have any idea who this is? Guess what? It's my brother!"

I took off my mask.

The woman dressed as a sixties flower child said:

"Oh, brother, put your mask back on."

Everybody laughed.

Medina was funny! I'll never forget her first words to me. *Oh brother, put your mask back on.*

At the time, Medina was raising her daughter, Jessica, on her own. She wanted her daughter to someday go to college but had nothing saved. As a single parent, it was always a struggle to make ends meet. With the dad out of the picture, I felt that tug of responsibility.

"Just give me time," I told her after we had been dating a while. "I will figure out a way to make this work. Jessica will go to college."

And she did.

Growing up, I was the only boy in a family of girls. My dad had left when I was six years old, and my stepdad worked night shifts, so I didn't see him much, either. This meant I learned a lot from the strong women around me.

My sisters, who were quite a bit older than me, each made their own choices in life. Watching them, I started to understand how people sometimes repeat what's familiar, even if these aren't the best patterns to repeat.

I realized I wanted to do things differently, especially for my stepdaughter. I wanted to show her that it's important to make good choices and to not just *go with what you know*. This hit me one day when I was about to leave for work. I had just had a small argument with Medina about how much time I spent with my friends.

Then, as I was taking Jessica to school, it suddenly clicked. It was like someone grabbed me by the lapels, gave me a good shake, and said, "If you're going to do this, then it is your responsibility to make sure these two ladies are well taken care of so that they never feel fear and uncertainty again."

That's the day I started to take my job and my role in the family very seriously.

I chose to set aside my own small, trivial desires—those simple, somewhat childish things I wanted—to ensure that Jessica and Medina could have the best life possible.

I'm telling you all this because that's the kind of adviser I am—everything I say, I mean it. I'm coming at this from a genuine place. I know how important it is to take care of your people, of loved ones who are important in your life. I know what it's like to have family relying on you, and I know how stressful it can be, managing these financial decisions alone. This chapter is here to give you a solid and easy strategy to help you navigate these choices.

Allow me to introduce you to the *Three Worlds of Money*.

Fast Fact: *According to a report by FINRA, investor knowledge in the United States is low.*[33]

HOW TO EVALUATE YOUR INVESTMENTS

The financial landscape has been rapidly evolving over the last 50 years to adjust to the fundamental shift in the retirement system. Not only are you now responsible for saving and investing, but you must also choose from among a greater array of increasingly complex financial products and instruments. This is no easy task.

New research conducted by the FINRA Investor Education Foundation and the Global Financial Literacy Excellence Center (GFLEC) at the George Washington University School of Business finds that the average saver has "alarmingly low" levels of financial knowledge.[34] The result? Low confidence when making investing decisions.

This matters because, as we discussed, the closer you get to the time of retirement, the more your financial goals begin to change. Asset allocation, risk tolerance, and financial needs all undergo a shift, and you need to know

---

[33] Lin, Judy T, et al, Investors in the United States: The Changing Landscape, FINRA, December 2022, page 2, Choice of Financial Adviser Can Dramatically Affect Retirement Savings, December 2022 https://finrafoundation.org/sites/finrafoundation/files/NFCS-Investor-Report-Changing-Landscape.pdf Accessed 12/28/2023.

[34] Williams, Angelita, and Rote, Mike, New Research: Many U.S. Investors With Low Financial Literacy Levels Are Ill-Equipped to Manage Personal Finances, Especially Investments, FINRA, October 2019, https://www.finra.org/media-center/newsreleases/2019/many-us-investors-ill-equipped-manage-personal-finances-especially Accessed 12/28/2023.

how to respond intelligently so that you can make informed decisions about whether these financial instruments are still what you need to achieve your goals.

Before we get into the mechanics of the *Three Worlds of Money*, it's helpful to know how to evaluate these worlds in terms of what they can give you. That way, whether you are in the late stages of saving for retirement or the early stages of life without work, you can choose intelligently.

While the types of assets in these worlds can get complicated, what they can do for you can be boiled down to three basic characteristics:

1. **Safety**
2. **Liquidity**
3. **Return**

Every investor, whether they know it or not, is always looking for these three things. Let's take a look at each of these characteristics and what they can do for you in retirement.

SAFETY

Safety refers to the protection of your principal. This is the initial amount you put into an investment. Is this amount guaranteed? Ask your adviser. In many cases, the answer is no. In other cases, the answer is yes, but with a cost. And then there are products where the safety is guaranteed, based on the strength of the issuing company, which means you need to do your research.

You don't want to keep your entire portfolio in safety, even during retirement. **Inflation risk** and healthcare needs require that your accounts still grow to meet these future demands. We already saw how these threats can derail a retirement. Balance is key.

What else do you need safety for? Income! You will want to know that the amount of money you need to pay the bills during retirement cannot suddenly disappear. This amount must be stable. Most people know how much they need each month to pay the bills, and if you don't, an adviser can help you figure this part out. Safety is imperative because you need to know that, even if the market tanks or a pandemic breaks out, you can still pay your rent, buy fresh fruit, and take your spouse out to a Halloween party.

LIQUIDITY

Liquidity refers to the ease and speed with which an asset can be converted to cash, without significantly altering its market value or incurring fees and penalties. In other words, it's not just about how quickly you can sell an asset, but also how much of its value you retain in the process.

You don't need to keep your entire portfolio liquid, even during retirement. You already know how to do this. During your working years, it's likely that you contributed to a tax-deferred retirement account that was largely illiquid—remember the rules for saving in an IRA or 401(k)? Pulling funds out early, before age 59½, would trigger a 10 percent IRS penalty. This was acceptable because those funds were designated for your *later* years.

Similarly, in retirement, you're planning not just for today, but for *your later years*. When you stop drawing a paycheck, you still have a future. The decisions you made in your 20s and 30s are the reasons this money is here for you today. Now, you're making decisions that your 75-year-old self will thank you for.

Are you going to do the right things?

Allocating some of your portfolio to less liquid assets with early withdrawal penalties is still a viable strategy, as long as you maintain sufficient liquid assets for your immediate needs.

What do you need liquid assets for? Primarily, they serve as an income replacement, supplemented by Social Security and possibly a pension. Your investment accounts may also provide additional income. Secondly, you need a liquid emergency fund to handle life's unexpected challenges. Finally, and perhaps most enjoyably, liquid assets enable you to fund the activities that make retirement truly fulfilling—be it travel, hobbies, or other lifelong dreams. After years of hard work, maintaining a level of liquidity ensures you can fully relish your retirement.

Fast Fact: *Research suggests that if you plan to travel and lead an active lifestyle, then you'll need to ratchet up your retirement budget by 6%.*[35]

---

[35] Fidelity Viewpoints, How much will you spend in retirement? Nov 2023, https://www.fidelity.com/viewpoints/retirement/spending-in-retirement Accessed 1/05/2024.

RETURN

Return refers to a measure of profit earned by your money. It's impossible to discuss return in retirement without also addressing risk. Are you comfortable with the amount you could lose in exchange for the amount you could earn?

We have already discussed why it's unwise to keep your entire portfolio exposed to the full powers of market loss once you near or enter retirement. The mathematical realities of account value restoration and sequence risk have shown us how factors completely out of our control can quickly devastate a retirement dream, turning it into a nightmare reality.

You don't have control over what the market does, but you DO have control over where to allocate this money. Putting 100 percent of your income in the stock market wasn't something you did during your working years, and it certainly isn't something you should be doing in retirement.

You need growth to maintain future expenses. What rate of return do you need to sustain your income? A moderately low rate is ideal because the chances are good that we can sustain it. Being completely risk averse can be a recipe for disaster.

On the other hand, having too hearty an appetite for risk can also spell disaster. If you don't have enough savings and your expenses are high, we might need to take on more risk to get the rate of return you need. Either you stomach more risk or figure out a way to reduce expenses. The strategy is completely driven by the customer. We make our recommendations, and then you have a response.

The other day, I presented a *Three Worlds of Money* plan to a client, and he said this to me:

"I still want to grow more. This projection shows me dying with half a million. I want to die with a full $1 million."

"We can do that," I replied. "But understand—by taking on this much risk, you're giving me permission to lose that money."

He thought about what that would mean.

"Never mind," he said. "I don't want to give you permission to lose my money. Let's do it the other way."

Working with an adviser who understands the risk associated with your timeline gives you a lot of flexibility. Within the *Three Worlds of Money*, there are a lot of different ways to get what you need.

Fast Fact: *According to an EBRI report, 74% of Americans worry that the stock market will be increasingly volatile and unpredictable.*[36]

THE 3 WORLDS OF MONEY

The inspiration for *The Three Worlds of Money* concept came from someone just like you. Our founder Gene Wittstock was in a conversation with a new client from Ann

---

[36] Retirement Confidence Survey, 2023, EBRI, https://www.ebri.org/docs/default-source/rcs/2023-rcs/2023-rcs-short-report.pdf Page 21, Accessed 12/04/2023.

Arbor. During this meeting, she made a straightforward yet pivotal statement:

"Forget all the fancy stock options, I want that Safe Money."

Gene didn't realize it then, but that phrase would become the seed from which *The Three Worlds of Money* concept would grow.

Given the innovation of today's new investment products, advisers find it difficult to break down your options neatly into categories like bank products, market investments, and insurance. We're seeing a lot of crossovers. Some bank investments are illiquid. Variable annuities are a type of insurance contract and yet they're not safe. Even market investments are offering structured notes and buffered ETFs that provide decent protection.

In our experience, what we realized is that every investor is looking for the same things from their investments.

1. **Safety:** How much of my money is safe if there is a serious market decline?
2. **Growth:** How much of my money is earning when there is strong growth potential in the market?
3. **Liquidity:** How much money can I access easily with no additional fees or costs and without the risk of losing money during a down market?

The problem is, we cannot get all three of these characteristics from one single investment, or even one single financial world! That's why we have THREE *Worlds of Money*. Each of these worlds is typically strong in two characteristics and weaker in the third. By combining money worlds, you can achieve true diversification with the access to safety, growth, and liquidity that you need.

We're not trying to sell you any single investment here—we are simply putting this into an eye-opening format for educational purposes. Most people when they plan using the *Three Worlds of Money* have an epiphany because they realize, "Wow, I see how I'm protected, and I see my earning potential. I also know where my income is coming from."

That is a powerful thing to have.

WORLD A: PROTECTION
Shielding Wealth in an Era of Extended Retirement.

Protected accounts offer the safety characteristic we described above. Examples might include fixed annuities, money market accounts, U.S. Treasury bonds, and good old-fashioned savings and checking accounts. We encourage our clients to use their bank for emergency funds.

We do not typically recommend bank CDs because they only support one of the three characteristics—safety. Bank CDs charge penalties if you withdraw the money early, which negates their liquidity. Furthermore, the growth they offer doesn't typically keep up with inflation. After paying taxes on the earnings, you want to have enough of a profit to at least help you stay ahead.

Thankfully, the world of protection has been growing in recent years, so you might have tools available to you that you haven't heard about yet. Below is a brief listing of three options along with the advantages and disadvantages of each.

FIXED ANNUITY

With a fixed annuity, you put a sum of money into the insurance agreement in exchange for an agreed-upon rate of return. These agreements are usually short term, from one to six years, but they could be as long as 10 years. If you break the terms of the agreement and take your money out early, you may face a surrender charge.

However, unlike a bank CD, fixed annuities typically allow you to withdraw up to 10 percent of your money annually without penalty.

Also, unlike a bank CD, fixed annuities grow tax-deferred. You do not have to report the interest earned on your annual tax return, so you do not have to pay taxes on the growth until you go to spend the money.

Advantages:
- Fixed interest rate.
- Safety and principal guarantees.
- No volatility or uncertainty.
- Interest accumulates tax-deferred.

Disadvantages:
- No access to market gains.
- Limited liquidity.
- Subject to inflation risk.

MONEY MARKET ACCOUNTS

A money market is an interest-bearing account that typically pays a higher interest rate than a regular savings account. As a bank product, the funds are FDIC-insured with the same account holder benefits typical of both savings and checking accounts. Money market savings accounts may require a higher balance than regular savings accounts to earn the higher interest rate, but funds are immediately accessible. This makes them a good place to store your cash reserves as part of a holistic retirement plan.

Advantages:
- Immediate liquidity.
- Higher interest rates than primary checking and savings.
- Safety with the guarantee of principal.
- FDIC-insured.

Disadvantages:
- No opportunity for market gains.
- Subject to inflation risk.
- Minimum balance may be required.

BANK CD

A certificate of deposit (CD) is a promissory note issued by a bank. The interest rate is fixed and your earnings are taxable. As compared to a bond, the durations are relatively short term, anywhere from six months to 10 years. And like a bank account, your funds are FDIC-insured.

The main disadvantage of bank CDs—and really any bank product—is that interest rates tend to be higher only during times of higher inflation. That makes it difficult to get ahead with these tools. Because we are currently in a low-interest-rate environment, retirees today are especially subject to inflation risk. Another thing to be aware of is the penalty you may pay for cashing in your CD early.

Advantages:
- Safety of principal.
- Fixed interest rate.
- No volatility or uncertainty.
- FDIC-insured.

Disadvantages:
- No opportunity for market gains.
- No liquidity.
- Subject to inflation risk.
- Earnings are taxed.

Fast Fact: *Research shows that fixed-rate deferred annuities average an interest rate over four times that of bank CDs.*[37]

---

[37] Annuities, Kiplinger, https://www.kiplinger.com/retirement/annuities#:~:text=%E2%80%9COur%20research%20shows%20fixed%2Drate,for%20protection%20and%20growth%20potential.%E2%80%9D, Accessed 1/09/2024.

WORLD B: POTENTIAL
Exploring the Landscape of Growth-Oriented Investments

Potential accounts offer the growth characteristic we described above. Examples might include stocks, bonds, investment funds, and variable annuities. Investors during their accumulation years can benefit from these products by using a passive, buy-and-hold approach, riding out the market highs and lows over time.

Investors with a shorter timeline may want to limit their exposure to market loss.

The **passive strategy** you relied on during your accumulation years operates under the assumption that you *must stay in the market* because you can't miss the best days. An **active strategy** operates under the directive to limit the worst days.

We already discussed how the investor with a shorter timeline doesn't have time to recover from market loss. The mathematical reality of account value restoration shows us why: we can never get back to even by receiving a gain equal to the loss. To combat this, we have money managers who use an active, **tactical strategy**.

An active strategy seeks to limit loss by ongoing buying and selling based on market conditions and economic indicators. Instead of receiving 100 percent of both gains and losses, the goal of an active strategy is to limit loss in exchange for a limited portion of the gains.

For example, an active strategy might seek to capture 70 percent of market gains and no more than 40 percent of market losses. You're still seeing a loss, but it's capped out and not bottomless.

An active management strategy gives specified objectives tailored to the investor at or nearing retirement. Your money is managed, meaning your holdings are actively adjusted. If the market is heading south, your money manager can move your holding to cash. This gives you help during times of volatility and the potential for improved risk-adjusted returns.

This strategy comes with a management fee in exchange for a shorter timeline and the peace of mind you get knowing someone is actually managing your money.

What follows are a handful of investments most common to the *Potential* money world. Any of these options can be used in either a passive or actively managed account. Some of these we recommend and others we do not. We have presented them here in an unbiased format so that you can decide for yourself what will help you best achieve your goals.

STOCKS

A stock is an equity position in a company. The first thing to know about your stock is whether it's common or preferred. Both types of stock are a tool that investors can use to profit from the future success of a business entity. **Common stocks** give shareholders voting rights while preferred stocks do not—but shareholders who own preferred stocks are given priority over a company's income and assets.

Secondly, stocks are named after the size of the company, small, mid, and large. To give you an idea of what that means, a small-cap stock would have a market capitalization of between $250 million and $2 billion, so we're not talking small fry. The geography of a stock is also a factor: domestic, international, or emerging markets. Stocks are also organized according to the sector they do business in—for example, healthcare, energy, or consumer staples.

And lastly, how does the corporation utilize the earnings? **Growth stocks** do not pay a dividend. When they make profits, the money goes back in to grow the company and investors see a capital appreciation in terms of the stock's value. On the opposite side of the spectrum, a **dividend stock** is where the money earned goes back to the shareholders. With dividend stocks, the company pays you to own it whether the stock goes up in value or not.

Advantages:
- Easy liquidity.
- Opportunities for growth.
- Hedges against inflation.

Disadvantages:
- No safety or guarantee of principal.
- Volatility and uncertainty.
- Things can change quickly.

INVESTMENT FUNDS

Mutual funds and exchange-traded funds (ETFs) are professionally managed pools of securities that rely on a buy-and-hold strategy. By pooling, investors with similar goals combine their savings to benefit from more diversification and lower individual risk. They invest (buy) in a diverse set of securities and keep (hold) that stock for a long period of time.

This is an example of a passive investment strategy where investors share in both the gains and losses.

A prospectus made available to all investors spells out the strategy and investment focus for the fund. One thing to note about the pooled fund philosophy is the 35d-1 rule. This rule does two things: 1) it prohibits a registered investment company from using a misleading fund name, and 2) it requires that the fund invest 80 percent of its assets in the type of security indicated by its fund name.[38]

So, what does that mean for you?

The very structure and philosophy of a mutual fund is the reason why the typical 401(k) or IRA loses money during market declines. Even when your fund manager is aware of approaching market volatility, he or she is legally required to stay invested in their assigned asset classes according to rule 35d-1.

---

[38] U.S. Securities and Exchange Commission, Fact Sheet: Amendments to the Fund "Names Rule," https://www.sec.gov/files/ic-34593-fact-sheet.pdf Accessed 12/28/2023.

When you invest in mutual funds, you are relying on a buy-and-hold strategy, and so you participate in the market lows as well as the market highs.

Advantages:
- Easy liquidity.
- Opportunity for returns.
- Easy diversification.

Disadvantages:
- No safety or guarantee of principal.
- Volatility and uncertainty.
- Professional management fees, trade costs, and marketing fees.
- Tax consequences can be hard to control.

Fast Fact: *From 1953 to 1981 in a generally increasing interest rate environment, the average annual return for all bonds was 2.48%. From 1981 to 2018 in a generally decreasing interest rate environment, the average annual return for all bonds was 9.95%.*[39]

---

[39] Damodaran, Aswath, Annual Returns on Stock, T.Bonds, and T.Bills: 1928 – Current, New York University, January 2024, http://pages.stern.nyu.edu/~adamodar/New_Home_Page/datafile/histretSP.html Accessed 1/09/2024.

BONDS

A bond is a debt investment in which you are financing an activity. You loan money to an entity for a defined period of time in exchange for a fixed amount of interest. The entity issues you a bond, and as such they are known as the issuer.
- If the issuer is the U.S. government, then you're buying treasury bonds where the interest is taxed as ordinary income.
- If the issuer is a state or local government, then you're buying municipal or muni bonds where the interest is not taxable. However, this interest is counted against you when configuring how much taxes you will pay on your Social Security income.
- If the issuer is a company, then you're buying a **corporate bond**. With a bond, you do not own equity in the company, so if they run into financial trouble, the company still has a legal obligation to pay you the promised interest rate. On the flip side, if the company becomes successful and profits soar, you won't receive more than the promised bond rate.

Bonds are usually thought of as the stable part of your typical stock and bond portfolio, to be purchased as part of a good diversification strategy against market volatility. But during your retirement years, bonds can expose you to risk if you need to sell them.

Because bonds have an inverse relationship with interest rates, they carry **interest rate risk**. When interest rates fall, bond prices rise; when interest rates rise, bond prices fall. We are currently experiencing a changing interest rate environment, and there is only one direction that bond prices can go. What does this mean for the investor entering retirement who is relying too heavily on bonds?

If you have to sell your bonds for income, then you may have to sell your bond for less than what you paid for it.

Federal Funds Effective Interest Rate (represents interest rates)

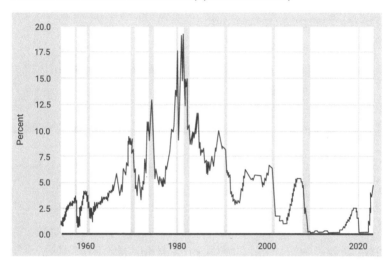

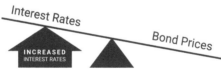

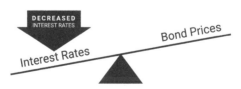

Source: Board of Governors of the Federal Reserve System

Advantages:
- Fixed interest rate.
- Referred to as fixed-income securities.

Disadvantages:
- Limited liquidity.
- Interest rate can be variable.
- May lose principal during changing interest rate environment.

Fast Fact: *The average fees for a variable annuity are 2.3% of the contract value, and these fees can be more than 3% annually.*[40]

VARIABLE ANNUITY

A variable annuity is one kind of **annuity** that offers you mutual funds wrapped inside an insurance vehicle. This gives you options for income generation and income protection, but your principal is *not* guaranteed. You are still taking 100 percent of the market risk while paying the highest fees for any annuity around, and that includes both one-time fees and an ongoing M&E risk fee.

Variable annuities do offer the same benefits of all annuities: they grow tax-deferred and can be passed to your heirs without **probate**. But variable annuities do not have the same principal guarantees as other annuities, and withdrawals can impact the income guarantees.

[40] Schell, Jennifer, Annuity Fees, and Commissions, Annuity.org, February 2023, https://www.annuity.org/annuities/fees-and-commissions/ Accessed 3/20/2023.

Advantages:
- Options for market returns.
- Tax-deferred growth.
- Income production options.
- Avoids probate.

Disadvantages:
- No guarantee of principal.
- Limited liquidity.
- Volatility and uncertainty.
- High fees.

WORLD C: HYBRID

Standing the Line Between Growth and Safety

A hybrid is a mixture of two different things. In this Money World, those two things are a blend of safety and growth. Investments like Equity-Based CDs, Indexed Universal Life Insurance, Fixed-Index Annuities, Buffered ETFs, and Structured Notes often make up this category.

These instruments commonly tie their performance to a market index, allowing for upside potential while also providing a cushion against market downturns. Although each has its own set of advantages and disadvantages, including varying degrees of liquidity with caps on potential gains, they can play a valuable role in a diversified portfolio aimed at achieving a well-rounded retirement strategy.

Hybrid options take more time to explain as they have multiple working parts. Below is a brief rundown on the mechanics of two of these options, along with the advantages and disadvantages of each.

FIXED-INDEXED ANNUITY

This type of deferred annuity is a combination of the variable annuity and the fixed annuity together. It really is a hybrid because it can give you a place to accumulate money for retirement while also preserving your income. The two parts of the fixed-indexed annuity to pay attention to are 1) the fixed principal guarantees and 2) the potential for market-linked returns.

First, you'll receive a principal guarantee. The amount of money you roll over into this vehicle is guaranteed not to go down due to stock market loss. This can be a valuable benefit for someone nearing retirement with an amount of money they know they need to use for income.

And second, you have the opportunity to hedge against inflation via market-linked returns. The indexing system allows you to track a market index without putting your money directly into the market. Gains are typically limited, so while you may not see double-digit returns, you will not earn anything less than 0 percent.

Indexed annuities do not credit you with a negative return, so even if the market falls, your account balance stays level.

Indexed annuities also have no fees unless you elect to purchase a rider, and most of them allow you to access your money without penalty should you have a long-term care event. The downside is that indexed annuities are typically long-term agreements of seven to 10 years. While you can access up to 10 percent of your money annually, you may be assessed a surrender charge should you go over that amount during the contract time.

Advantages:
- Fixed interest rate.
- Safety and principal guarantees.
- Access to market-linked interest.
- Tax-deferred growth.
- Guaranteed income.
- No loss due to market volatility.
- Protection against longevity risk.
- Access to liquidity during a long-term care event.

Disadvantages:
- Limited liquidity unless there is a long-term care event.
- Longer investment timeline.

Fast Fact: *Research finds that most retirees would be better off if they had access to deferred income annuities as evidenced by a 15-20% improvement in their financial well-being.*[41]

INDEXED UNIVERSAL LIFE

The goal of an IUL policy is the opposite of a traditional life insurance policy. Instead of paying a *lower* amount of

---

[41] Parameshwaran, Shankar, Why Retirement Gets Better With Annuities, Knowledge at Wharton, Wharton School of the University of Pennysalvania, Jan 2024, https://knowledge.wharton.upenn.edu/article/why-retirement-gets-better-with-annuities/ Accessed 1/10/2024.

money for a *larger* death benefit, we're designing a policy with a *smaller* death benefit to achieve a *greater* cash accumulation value for your situation.

To do this, the IUL uses an indexing method for accumulation with principal protection features. This method is similar to the indexing system used by the fixed-indexed annuity. It can offer the potential for cash value accumulation *outside* of the stock market. Like a retirement savings vehicle, it offers tax-deferred growth, but you are funding this strategy with money you've already paid the taxes on. You cannot deduct these contributions come tax time, but that means you're free from the IRS rules about when and how to spend this money.

The tax savings offered by the IUL are considerable. There are no RMDs, and you don't have to wait until you are age 59 ½ before you spend it. The IUL can also offer additional tax savings for later when it is designed by an adviser who knows how to utilize this strategy.

The only caveat is that because these life insurance policies take time to build, it's best to wait a certain number of years before accessing the money so the strategy has time to go to work for you. Most people wait to access this money as additional income later in retirement.

The more you fund the policy, the more the build-up of the cash value, but it must be funded *in balance* with the death benefit. Its main prerogative is to do what good life insurance does: function as an estate planning tool that provides a tax-free death benefit to your family. But when you understand its internal benefits, that's when things can get exciting.

Advantages:
- Tax-free death benefit for your family.
- Tax-deferred accumulation.
- Principal protection from market fluctuations.
- Interest credits that never go below zero.
- Access to tax-free retirement money.
- No RMDs.
- Available at any age.

Disadvantages:
- Requires after-tax dollars to fund.
- Upfront fee structure.
- A long-term time horizon of seven to 10 years.
- Must be healthy to qualify.

Fast Fact: *Understanding of retirement plan options is lacking and many people don't consider their plan provider as a go-to source for information and advice.*[42]

HOW MUCH SHOULD YOU PUT IN EACH WORLD?

Last week I met with a gentleman named Earl who had a $1 million portfolio, and he was not happy with the service he

---

[42] Retirement Confidence Survey, 2023, EBRI, https://www.ebri.org/docs/default-source/rcs/2023-rcs/2023-rcs-short-report.pdf Page 8, Accessed 12/04/2023.

had received from his previous financial professional. That adviser had put all $1 million into ONE money world. Even worse—it was all sitting inside ONE type of product.

Earl was not diversified, the surrender period wasn't laddered, and he couldn't access his money to put a down payment on a beach condo. Furthermore, the adviser had not done any planning. All he had done was sell Earl a product. One product! Understandably, Earl was upset.

That is not what we are doing here. First, we always err on the side of caution. I ask people, "How much of your portfolio do you want to keep in liquidity?" Sometimes, I hear a low number.

"Oh, I only need $20,000."

I remind them: "This is retirement! Time to enjoy the fruit of your labor!"

People tend to spend more money early on in retirement, filling this new amount of time they now have with activities that cost money—going to shows, taking trips, or buying a beach house. And this is wonderful, but we must be careful to fund the plan properly, and we must know, from a tax standpoint, where we will get this money and how much it will really cost us.

Our firm was able to help Earl to reverse the mistake his previous adviser made. Using the 10 percent free withdrawals that came with that particular product, we slowly but surely moved his money into another more diversified plan. Keeping the plan flexible is important. If you decide to buy a beach condo six months into retirement, we want you to have a plan that can accommodate those kinds of spontaneous decisions.

This is why part of our planning process includes a period of time where we get to know you and how you spend. Are you spontaneous? Or a creature of habit? Do you still have kids living with you? If so, what are their ages? By asking questions like this, we always find things that can help you do more with what you have. We also want to understand your liquidity needs and how much you need to live on—the bills you must pay and the loved ones you take care of. We can't just lock up all the money into accounts with surrender fees when you might need that money for unexpected situations before the account matures.

Another question I ask when ascertaining how much money to put into each *Money World* is about risk tolerance. How much loss can you actually stomach? I like to remind people that, yes, the ocean is warm and blue and nice to swim in. It's okay to go in there, but ... you must keep an eye out for the sharks.

Some people have no interest in swimming with sharks. The only program that is guaranteed not to lose no matter what happens is the *Protected World*. As your adviser, I could be asleep, and that account would have an auto-braking feature if the market turns. There is a way to help determine how much of your portfolio to allocate there. That formula, along with the most common income-producing vehicles offered by this world, are what we will discuss next.

At the end of the day, I can't make a recommendation about how much you should put into each world. I would first have to know who you are and what you're trying to accomplish. Some people may be able to find the safety, growth, and liquidity they need in the *Hybrid World* alone. Others will find that they need to have a portion of their savings in the *Potential World* to capitalize on the growth opportunities during bull markets. The only way to know for sure what you need is to have your individual situation analyzed by a competent financial team.

CHANGE YOUR MINDSET: NEXT STEPS
REALLY DO YOUR PLANNING.

- Having explored the *Three Worlds of Money*—Potential, Protection, and Hybrid—you're now armed with the knowledge to create a well-rounded retirement portfolio.
- Take the first step toward a secure financial future by crafting a plan that's specifically tailored to you.
- Contact us for a no-obligation, customized retirement consultation today where we can put the *Three Worlds of Money* method into action.
- Call us at 1-866-QUEST-01.
- For Michigan residents, call 248-599-1000.
- Visit us at 30700 Telegraph Rd, Ste 1475, Bingham Farms, MI, 48025.

STEP 4

CHOOSE THE RIGHT VEHICLE FOR THE JOB

RACE CAR, STATION WAGON, OR SUV

"You must convert wealth into income at retirement."

~ Moshe A. Milevsky, Ph.D.

I was at the Home Depot the other day when I saw this guy buying sod. He was probably doing some landscaping work for a new house he was building because he had a few rolls of it. But what made me stop and take notice was when he unloaded these rolls and put them into the back of his car, which happened to be a Mercedes.

A Mercedes-Benz AMG GT R Coupe.

Yup. This guy was putting *sod* into a $150,000 car.

He was getting dirt and debris all over his posh leather seats because he was literally using the wrong vehicle for the job. Why not borrow your nephew's clunker? Use the old pickup sitting in the garage? Anything. *Anything* would be better than using the fastest rear-wheel-drive road-going sports car ever tested!

Maybe I am getting too excited here, but it's a lot of fun to make this comparison because in so many ways the analogy is perfect:

You want to be very careful when choosing the investment vehicles you drive into retirement.

Is the Mercedes a bad vehicle? Absolutely not! It's wonderful! Who wouldn't want to drive one? But you want to use it for the right thing—such as driving out to the beach with the top down to make all your friends jealous. It might not be the right vehicle to drive you through retirement, however. Here's why:

Once you shift gears into distribution mode, the goal of your investments is to replace the paycheck you once received from working. That requires a very specific kind of financial vehicle. Social Security only replaces about 40 percent of the average worker's pre-retirement income, and experts suggest you will need 70 to 85 percent or more of pre-retirement earnings to live comfortably.[43] Where is the rest of the income going to come from?

For most of us, the answer has to do with tax-deferred accounts like the 401(k). But what is a 401(k)? It's not a pension, it's not a paycheck, it's not even a guarantee. It's a collection of investments vulnerable to stock market volatility.

You might compare these stock market investments to driving a race car when heading into retirement. Yes, they have some impressive horsepower under the hood, but—how safe will your income be if you're relying 100

---

[43] Social Security Administration, Understanding the Benefits, 2024, https://www.ssa.gov/pubs/EN-05-10024.pdf Accessed 1/10/2024.

percent on market performance? Race cars don't even have headlights! They're designed to go very fast, and there's no room for the wife, the kids, and the family dog.

On the other end of the spectrum, we have your *Protected World* options. These vehicles are like the family station wagon—they can haul around everything, including sod. They are reliable, dependable, but not necessarily sexy. If your mom made you learn how to drive using the family wagon, then you probably felt very uncool, albeit safe.

There is a third option available for retirees today. This third option comes from the *Hybrid World*, but they offer you the same guarantees as the *Protected World* of money. They also offer you the opportunity for market-linked returns without direct exposure in the market itself. That's a pretty nifty vehicle. You might even compare it to the SUV—roomy, reliable, and aerodynamic enough not to embarrass your teenage son.

Before you choose your vehicle, however, we first have to talk about fuel efficiency—AKA, a spending plan. Your first assignment when figuring this out is to identify how much income you require this financial vehicle to provide.

Fast Fact: *Fewer than two-thirds of workers are confident they know how much to withdraw from their savings and investments in retirement.*[44]

---

[44] Retirement Confidence Survey, 2023, EBRI, page 10, https://www.ebri.org/docs/default-source/rcs/2023-rcs/2023-rcs-short-report.pdf Accessed 1/10/2024.

IDENTIFY YOUR INCOME GAP

To identify your **income gap** in retirement, first, estimate your anticipated monthly expenses, including essentials like housing, utilities, healthcare, and food, as well as discretionary spending such as travel and entertainment. Ideally, you want to track your spending for three to four months. Additionally, when assessing your expenses, it's beneficial to distinguish between your *needs* and *wants*.

Needs encompass essential expenditures like housing, utilities, and healthcare. These are the things required by the body for basic survival.

- Food
- Water
- Shelter
- Utilities
- Insurance
- Clothing
- Healthcare
- Medicine/prescriptions
- Transportation

Wants include discretionary spending such as dining out, travel, and entertainment. Wants might be essential to the mind and spirit, but they are things the body could live without.

- Travel
- Vacations
- Hobbies
- Charitable donations

- Grandchildren spoiling
- New cars
- Dining out
- RV expenses

Look at what you are currently spending every month in the six areas of housing, healthcare, transportation, personal insurance, food, and miscellaneous expenses. Here is a breakdown of these six areas to give you an idea of what kinds of things you should include in each category.

Housing: includes mortgage cost, property taxes, homeowner's insurance, rent, utilities, repairs, maintenance, plus other fees and expenses.

Healthcare: includes medical services, medications, and supplies, plus health insurance.

Transportation: includes vehicle maintenance, fuel, auto insurance, public transportation, and rideshare expenses.

Personal Insurance: includes life insurance, umbrella policies, disability insurance, long-term care, final expenses, or any other insurance.

Food: includes both groceries and dining out.

Miscellaneous: includes outstanding loan payments, credit card payments, entertainment, travel and vacation, hobbies, gifts, education expenses, charitable donations, and any other expenses not listed.

Next, tally up your expected income streams—Social Security, pensions, and any other regular income you anticipate. The **income gap** is the difference between your retirement living expenses and the income from guaranteed sources such as pensions or Social Security.

Living expenses - guaranteed income
= the income gap

Once you subtract your total expected income from your estimated monthly expenses, you will have a known income gap that needs to be filled. This gap represents the amount you'll want to generate from your investment portfolio or other financial vehicles to maintain your desired lifestyle in retirement. Knowing your income gap is crucial for tailoring an investment strategy that aligns with your financial needs and goals.

Fast Fact: *Plan on approximately 15% of your retirement expenses to be related to health care; the more health issues you expect, the higher the income replacement rate you'll want to work into your plan.*[45]

---

[45] Fidelity Viewpoints, How Much Will You Spend in Retirement? Fidelity, November 2023, https://www.fidelity.com/viewpoints/retirement/spending-in-retirement Accessed 1/10/2024.

FILL YOUR INCOME GAP

The ideal vehicle for filling your income gap should share many similar characteristics with Social Security. It will keep up with inflation, it will be safe and protected, and it will last as long as you do.

It's crucial to factor in inflation when projecting your future income needs, as the purchasing power of your money will likely decrease over time. Social Security provides you with an *increasing* income to help address inflation risk. Legislation enacted in 1973 gives a **cost-of-living adjustment** (COLA) to your benefit. This means **your payments are designed to help keep pace with inflation**. Based on the increase in the Consumer Price Index for Urban Wage Earners and Clerical Workers (CPI-W), the COLA for 2023 was 8.7 percent; the highest ever COLA was 14.3 percent in 1980; the COLA for 2024 is 3.2 percent.[46] Over the course of a 20-year retirement, these increases can really add up.

If Social Security includes a pay increase, shouldn't your income plan include one, too? Ignoring inflation can lead to a serious miscalculation of your income gap, potentially jeopardizing your financial well-being in retirement.

Safety is important because, while it might be possible to adjust your spending by going without your *wants*, your income *needs* must be met no matter the economic weather. Should you find it necessary to adjust your spending to close the income gap, start by evaluating your

---

[46] Social Security Administration, Cost-of-Living Adjustment (COLA) Information for 2024, https://www.ssa.gov/cola/ Accessed 1/10/2024.

wants category. This enables you to make more informed and less painful financial adjustments while ensuring that your essential *needs* are still met.

And finally, you want this vehicle to last a lifetime and not conk out when you've still got miles of road left. If you are married, then you'll also want this income to continue for your spouse. Not even Social Security does that.

There is a vehicle in the financial industry designed specifically to solve the problem of lifetime income in retirement. It can even take care of your spouse. The only problem with it is that there's been a lot of bad press out there about these vehicles.

SPIDERS & ANNUITIES: WHY PEOPLE HATE THEM

Yes, I'm talking about annuities.

An annuity is the only financial product capable of turning a sum of money into a guaranteed lifetime income for retirement.[47]

That income can be designed to last 10 years, five years, 20 years, or the rest of your life. You get to choose. They even have annuities for married couples that can be set to extend the income to whomever lives the longest, no matter how long that person lives.

And yet you hear stories about advisers who *hate* them. You see advertisements and listicles, "10 Reasons Why I Hate Annuities and You Should Too." If one adviser tells

---

[47] Guarantees are based on the financial strength of the issuing company.

you they're good and another tells you they are bad, who is telling the truth?

This is why I'm so passionate about this vehicle analogy—it's so perfect! The answer is clear:

You must choose the financial vehicle based on what you're trying to do.

If you're chasing returns and saving for retirement, then a race car is probably best. The adviser who sells you the race car isn't selling you a bad car—it just might not be safe enough to drive all the way through retirement.

Look—I'm not going to tell you that annuities aren't dangerous. They're like spiders—a lot of people are afraid of them. There are more than 43,000 different kinds of spiders in the spider world, and of those, less than one-tenth of one percent have ever been responsible for a human death.[48] Now, isn't that reassuring? Doesn't knowing that make you like spiders more?

Haha—probably not. If you're a person who is afraid of spiders, you're still going to be wary of them. And that's okay. We can work with that. A certain amount of caution is warranted when choosing an annuity because these are long-term vehicles. You're going to be driving this car for a while, so you definitely want to take it out for a test spin. There are a ton of annuity programs out there, maybe not 43,000, but A LOT. Some are good for some people and others are bad for some people.

So, let's talk now about how to recognize an annuity that won't bite you.

---

[48] Rafferty, John P, 9 of the World's Deadliest Spiders, Britannica, https://www.britannica.com/list/9-of-the-worlds-deadliest-spiders Accessed 10/19/2023.

HOW TO CHOOSE THE RIGHT VEHICLE FOR THE JOB

Typically, annuities are long-term insurance tools with limited access to liquidity. This makes it vital that you **choose an annuity program that's designed to DO what you need it to do.** Shop around, kick the tires, and compare different insurance companies to get the benefits and features best suited to your needs. You'll want to ask yourself a couple of important questions:

- *When* do you need the income?
- For *how long* do you need the income?
- *Who* do you need this income for?
- *How much* income do you require?
- Do you need this income to *increase* over time?

Your answers to those five questions should dictate the vehicle you choose—not some article on some adviser's blog that wasn't even written for you. Keep that in the front of your mind and remember what YOU are trying to do. The solution will be different for each person. This will help you determine what kind of annuity to buy. There are a few things to keep in mind when answering the first question.

WHEN DO YOU NEED THE INCOME?

The kind of programs that I help people get into are designed to generate income *when* you need it. You get to choose payment terms, and depending on the type of annuity, your income can be set to arrive monthly, annually, quarterly, or even as a lump-sum deposit. In simplest terms, deciding *when* comes down to a question of *now* or *later*.

- Do you want to start generating your retirement income right now?
- Or do you want to wait a few years?

In the annuity world, there are two main types: immediate and deferred.

IMMEDIATE ANNUITIES

As the name suggests, if you need the retirement income right *now*, then an immediate annuity will likely be the right choice. You might think of this type of annuity as the station wagon. It's a bit sluggish. It has wood paneling and was the kind of wagon that Ward Cleaver drove from the sitcom from *Leave it to Beaver*.

The immediate annuity has liquidity disadvantages, it's not very flexible, and you must pay very close attention to your election decisions if you're trying to pass this money on to your family or spouse. Any leftover funds may, or may *not* pass to your beneficiaries, depending on the product. But the biggest disadvantage to be aware of is this:

Once you put your money into this type of annuity vehicle, you no longer have access to the lump sum. At the end of the day, it's just not as flexible as other types of annuities. Thankfully, better options exist if you do a little planning.

DEFERRED ANNUITIES

If retirement is five or more years away and you want to preserve your income, or you want to set aside some money in the *Protected World* to access later in life, a **deferred annuity** might be the type of vehicle that you need. Of the deferred annuities, there are two main kinds:

- The variable annuity
- The fixed-indexed annuity

For a refresher on the advantages and disadvantages of each, refer to Step Three where we talked about the variable annuity and the fixed-indexed annuity. As they relate to the income you need, here's what you'll want to know:

Variable annuities are like race cars: they do NOT protect you from risk. The amount of your principal is still not guaranteed, even if you purchase riders and special income options to guarantee the income. What you are paying for can be had for a much lower cost without all the fees. The type of vehicle that I would recommend instead is the fixed-indexed annuity.

If you've been reading along with me so far, then you'll remember the story I told about our CEO and founder, Gene Wittstock. (If you're one of those people who skip introductions—go back and read this!) When Gene was looking for a solution for his ladies from Detroit, what he found was the fixed-index annuity. But his brokerage firm didn't offer them because a fixed-index annuity is not a security. It doesn't fall under the umbrella of a stock market investment, it's not a race car, and so his firm was not able to get this type of vehicle for his ladies.

This, in a nutshell, is why so many advisers say, "I hate annuities"—they simply don't have access to the kind that you need.

A BRIEF ARGUMENT ABOUT ANNUITIES

The other day I got into a debate with a stock market guy about annuities. Now, the thing you have to understand is this: the only kind of annuity that most stock market guys can offer is a variable annuity. A variable annuity is a deferred annuity. A variable annuity is a race car annuity. A variable annuity falls under the umbrella of a market investment. Therefore, a variable annuity belongs in the *Potential World* of money. It does not belong in the *Protected World*.

That's why I do not recommend a variable annuity for your income needs.

Now, if you're going to a broker and you tell him you want an annuity for your retirement income, what's he going to say? The only kind of annuity that a broker can get you is a variable annuity. They cannot get you into a fixed-indexed annuity. That type of annuity just isn't on the menu.

That's why I got into this argument. The broker was saying bad things about *all* annuities.

"What's so bad about them?" I asked.

"They're really confusing and complex," he said.

"Okay, great," I said. "Explain a class B mutual fund in a way that's not confusing and complex. Explain why you charge a management fee of 1.5 or 3 percent. Explain why this is better than a class C or class D. Explain why the person who manages it also gets a backend fee. Explain why those fees aren't listed on the monthly statement?"

A fixed-indexed annuity isn't any more confusing. All financial programs come with disclosures and terms that aren't always easy to understand. What is actually happening inside a corporate bond? Most people have no idea, and yet, they own bonds.

Whenever I or anyone else at my firm recommends a financial vehicle for our client, we always explain it. We want to make sure that the client understands it. This is what I want you to know about what the fixed-indexed annuity can do.

WHAT THE FIXED-INDEX ANNUITY CAN DO

The fixed-index annuity (FIA) is the place to put future money for later use that you can't possibly lose. Let me say that again:

The money in a fixed-indexed annuity is future money for later use that you can't possibly lose.

This is a nest egg for later just like your 401(k) was a nest egg for later, only with the FIA, you can't lose the money. It's going to grow a little bit, and even if it's not in an IRA, it's still tax-deferred just like a retirement account.

What's especially nice about this type of deferred annuity is that you can put the same amount of money in it that you would have put into an immediate annuity, and then generate a *higher* income *later*. The reason for this has to do with the indexing feature. They can, generally speaking, get you more income for your hard-earned buck.

This is why I call these annuities the SUVs of the annuity world. They offer many hybrid features that combine the best of both money worlds: the *Potential* of a race car with market-linked returns, combined with the *Protection* and the safety features of the family station wagon. Indexed annuities might take longer to mature, but as long as you know that ahead of time, going into them, most people are willing to make the trade-off for the benefits they provide.

Those benefits are: principal protection, stock-market linked interest, access to your funds, low to no fees, and guaranteed income for later. Yes, these vehicles can produce income for life without an income rider or high fees. Yes, these vehicles can make sure that the income continues for your spouse. Yes, these vehicles were designed to beat or at least keep up with inflation. Yes, you can pass on any money not spent to your family—and without having to go through probate.

Fast Fact: *Nearly 90% of annuity owners worry less about retirement, and 75% say they have more money for discretionary spending because they own annuities.*[49]

---

[49] New York Life Research, June 2023, https://www.newyorklife.com/newsroom/annuity-owners-report-spending-more-staying-invested-and-feeling-happier-in-retirement Accessed 1/10/2024.

WHY ZERO IS YOUR HERO

Some investors don't need to know how the car works—they just like to drive. A fixed-indexed annuity is like that. I just told you what it can do—it gives you money for later. It can be designed with or without an income rider to generate a steady or increasing income for someone in retirement, for the rest of your life and the life of your spouse, if that's what you need. If you don't care how the engine works and you know how to work the headlights and auto-cruise, then head over to the end of the chapter and follow the next steps.

If you're curious and you want to peek under the hood, so to speak, to learn how these things work, then keep on reading here with me.

A fixed-indexed annuity can be very flexible. It doesn't just have to be used to create retirement income. This *money for later* can be used for anything. When it's designed correctly, it can function as a savings vehicle where you can accumulate funds without the risk of market loss, guaranteed.[50] Many of these annuities today also give you a way to pay for long-term care costs without having to buy extra insurance. There is no medical exam needed to qualify, and no extra riders to buy. Known as "income doublers," this benefit is automatically included with many of the *newer* types of deferred indexed annuities available today.

---

[50] Guarantees are backed by the financial strength of the claim's paying ability of the issuing company.

The way a fixed-indexed annuity accumulates while protecting your principal is a unique feature of the indexing system. This system allows it to *lock in* the earnings. This is a feature known as **annual reset**, and as the visual shows, this is what allows you to preserve and protect the money you have saved.

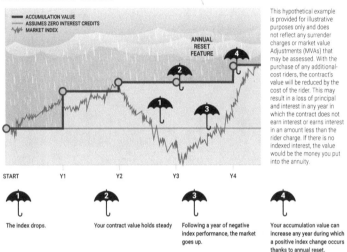

Most fixed-indexed annuities and indexed-universal life products undergo an annual reset on their anniversary date. During this reset, any accumulated gains are secured, shielding them from potential future market declines. This annual milestone also offers the chance to modify your indexing options. The concept of the "power of zero" highlights the ability of these products to preserve *both* your principal and any gains you've locked in, even when the market dips. This ensures that you don't have to recover from losses during market downswings; instead, any growth during market recovery directly translates into gains for your account.

To achieve this type of principal protection and lifetime income options, the insurance company needs time. As a deferred annuity, fixed-indexed annuities are typically longer contracts of seven or more years, so there are surrender charges to be aware of. Check out the visual here of an example schedule, and please note that annuities with different terms exist.

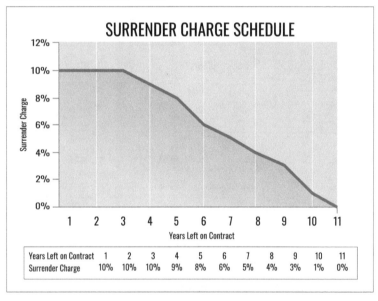

Source: Magellan Financial. Created for illustration purposes only and not representative of an actual product.

Regardless of the surrender schedule, it's always possible to completely avoid these charges. Just don't spend the money during the early years, and you won't be assessed the surrender charge. Simple as that.

The charges always go down the longer you hold the annuity, and all surrender schedules eventually end.

Some of them even start going down after the first year, and many carriers offer you 10 percent withdrawals—penalty free. When the contract matures, the surrender charges go away, and you are free to move the money to someplace else.

Surrender charges are easily avoided with the creation of an emergency fund within your *Protected World*. Most financial professionals recommend having three to six months' worth of income in an account you can easily access without fear of penalties, taxes, or market loss. A money market savings account is usually a good choice. By working with a financial professional who helps you keep track of RMDs, tax rules, and surrender charge schedules, you'll be able to enjoy the tax benefits of your annuity vehicle worry-free.

Regardless of what type you choose, *all* annuities grow tax-deferred and pass to your **beneficiary** without having to go through probate court. This makes them a valuable asset class for the retiree to have.

CHANGE YOUR MINDSET: NEXT STEPS
CHOOSE YOUR PRODUCT FROM THE *HYBRID WORLD*.

- Look at the characteristics of what the company is offering: What are the terms? Five percent versus .05 percent can add up to a lot of dollars during the course of a 20-year retirement.
- Look at a company's rating: How much money do they keep on hand to meet their debt obligations? The higher the rating, the stronger the financial strength of the company. This is important for the *Hybrid World* because principal guarantees are backed by the financial strength of the issuing company.
- Do they have a good program? Do you understand the surrender schedule? A good program will meet your financial objectives.

STEP 5

CONSIDER FUTURE TAX OBLIGATIONS

"An investment in knowledge pays the best dividends."

~ Benjamin Franklin

When Maureen retired at the age of 62, her best friend Mimi took her out to dinner. They went to the little Italian place on the corner where they served chianti by the glass. They toasted Maureen's retirement, and then, Maureen confessed to her friend that she was worried.

"I want to do the right thing with my money so that I don't run out," she said.

Mimi totally understood. While they were waiting for their entrees to arrive, Mimi told her about something called a Roth conversion that would lower her tax bill in retirement.

"You basically turn your taxable money into tax-free money," Mimi explained. "Anyone can do it. All you have to do is take out a certain amount of money from your regular IRA and put it into a Roth IRA. Then, when you need it later for income, presto! It's tax-free." She took another sip of her wine. "It significantly lowered my tax bill in retirement."

Maureen was intrigued.

"How does it work? How much money do you have to take out?"

"Just enough to stay under your current income tax bracket," Mimi explained. "Just figure out what your current rate is and take out enough to stay below that."

Their entrees arrived. The waiter poured them more wine.

"Why is it tax free?" Maureen asked, spreading the napkin out on her lap.

"Because that's just how a Roth IRA works. Any gains you make you get to keep completely tax free."

"Well, if they're so great, why doesn't everyone have one?"

"It's a little-known secret." Mimi raised her glass. "But now, you're in the know."

The two of them toasted their glasses again. Later, they ordered the tiramisu.

The next morning, Maureen thought about it again. She thought that tax-free income sounded pretty great, but she still wasn't clear about how the program worked. She had a ton of questions.

How did a person get into a Roth IRA?

When would she have to pay the taxes owed on her regular IRA?

And what were the limits and rules?

Maureen realized she needed to get some help if she was going to get this right. She found the name of a retirement planning firm that also worked with CPAs to consider taxes. Of course, that firm was us. She called Quest and set up her appointment. I'll never forget her first meeting because Maureen came to us so prepared.

"I want to do something called a Roth conversion," she explained to our team. Maureen had learned about her current income tax rate and had a number in mind to keep below the threshold. "I want to convert $40,000 this year from my **traditional IRA** into a Roth IRA so that I can lower my tax bill in retirement." She felt proud of herself for doing her homework and learning about this.

Our firm's CPA was also impressed.

"Taxes are the most important and overlooked aspect of retirement planning," he told her. "Most people don't even think about them."

"I have friends in high places," Maureen said sagely.

We all laughed.

"So—let's do this!" she said.

"Hold on," I spoke up. "We have to take a look at your entire situation first because there's a lot to consider."

"Like what?"

I asked her about her healthcare. Maureen had retired early at age 62, but Medicare didn't kick in until age 65.

"How are you getting your health insurance?" I inquired.

"The Marketplace."

"Okay. Let's take a look at that."

Our team did the calculations, and we learned that had she done the Roth conversion the way she wanted to, pulling out $40,000 in her first year, her monthly health insurance premiums would have increased significantly, so converting would have *cost* her money. The subsidies that the federal government gives towards medical coverage are income driven. Roth conversions increase income for the year the conversion took place.

Maureen sat back in her seat, stunned.

"Boy, am I glad I didn't act on this alone."

Once I had our firm's tax advisers look over Maureen's situation, we were able to devise a plan to convert her taxable income to tax-free income using a Roth conversion strategy designed to fit her. This strategy would take several years to implement in full, but it would go on to save her more than $120,000 in retirement.[51]

Fast Fact: *Income taxes can be your single largest expense in retirement.*[52]

THE TICKING TAX BOMB

Way back in Chapter Two we talked about how countless financial gurus preach the mantra: "Always tax-defer your retirement contributions because your earning years are your highest tax years." And yet, I've worked with countless individuals who are retired and currently shouldering a higher tax burden than they ever faced during their working years. Why is this happening?

---

[51] The above story uses fictional characters with actual figures from sources believed to be reliable. This example is shown for illustrative purposes only. Your results may vary.
[52] FINRA, Taxation of Retirement Income, 2023, https://www.finra.org/investors/learn-to-invest/types-investments/retirement/managing-retirement-income/taxation-retirement-income Accessed 12/28/2023.

The reality is, when you tax-defer a substantial portion of your retirement savings, you might inadvertently set a tax timer ticking away silently in the background. This sneaky timer detonates years later in the form of Required Minimum Distributions, or RMDs. These tax-deferred accounts continue to flourish and grow until RMDs compel us to start pulling out larger sums every year, inadvertently hiking up our tax obligations during our golden years.

Now, when we choose to tax-defer our retirement savings contributions, we're essentially entering into an agreement with the IRS.

They say, "Hey, you don't have to pay taxes on those contributions right now."

And we say, "Hey, that sounds great!"

It's a tempting offer because it lessens your tax burden during your working years. However, in exchange, the IRS also has a few stipulations.

First, they dictate that we can't access these funds before age 59 ½. And if we do? Well, you won't just owe money for the deferred taxes; you're also slapped with a 10 percent penalty. Remember what happened to Sabrina from our story in Step Two? That was based on a real-life scenario—I see these tax mishaps all the time, even from people who seek professional help.

In some cases, they are misled by their current adviser due to simple ignorance. Truth is, there are a lot of rules.

There are over 4.1 million words in the U.S. tax code—twice the number of words of all five *Game of Thrones* books combined.[53] I don't know all those rules, and I'm willing to bet neither does your current adviser. That's why we have tax professionals working with us at Quest.

Question is, does your current advisor work with a tax adviser? Or are they in competition for your business?

This is another side to the financial planning business that most people never consider, but that I ran into when I was in your shoes, and it nearly drove me mad. If no one is watching out for you, this is what happens:

Once you're comfortably settled into retirement with an investment plan all snuggly in place, your mid-70s come sneaking up on you in the night. Then if you don't start taking mandatory distributions at the pace the IRS dictates, they begin to nudge you—rather forcefully. They'll require you to begin *withdrawing money*, even if you don't want to. Even if you don't need those funds, they will require that you take the money out just so they can tax it.

What am I talking about? The notorious Required Minimum Distributions, or RMDs, that we mentioned earlier. Did you know that the percentage you must take out—and consequently *pay tax on*—only grows with each passing year? As you're getting older and not spending as much, they will insist you spend money from this growing account.

---

[53] Kiernan, John S, 2023 Tax Facts Infographic, Wallet Hub, March 2023, https://wallethub.com/blog/tax-day-facts/11835 Accessed 5/08/2023.

This often catches retirees off guard. Those pesky Required Minimum Distributions can potentially escalate the tax rate on the entirety of your assets for a particular year. It's like a ripple effect: the RMDs don't just influence the immediate funds you withdraw; they can also impact other crucial aspects of your retirement!

Taking an IRA distribution no matter how big or small will increase your annual income. This has the potential to set off the following:

- An increase to your marginal tax rate.
- An increase in the amount of overall income taxes you pay.
- An increase in the amount of your Social Security benefit that is taxable.
- An increase to your Medicare Parts B and D premiums.

How much will your taxes go up? Crossing over the threshold into a new marginal tax rate can increase your overall tax bill by as much as 83 percent under current law. However, current rates are scheduled to change. The Tax Cuts and Jobs Act of 2017 resulted in lower tax rates for millions of Americans. Unless Congress takes action, this act is set to expire at the end of 2025, and when it does, tax rates will revert to 2017 levels. We will be discussing next how this could result in an increase in taxes for a majority of Americans.[54]

---

[54] Schmitz Jr., Joe F., What You Can Do Now to Avoid Paying Higher Taxes in 2026, Kiplinger, Dec 2023, https://www.kiplinger.com/taxes/avoid-paying-higher-taxes-in-2026-what-you-can-do-now Accessed 1/17/2024.

Another thing that the RMD affects is the taxes owed on your Social Security. How much in taxes will you pay on this income benefit? It's determined by something termed *provisional income*. Now, if your income starts *increasing* because of other streams, say pensions or—you guessed it—withdrawals from tax-deferred accounts like an IRA, then the taxes you owe on your Social Security benefits follows suit. And it doesn't stop there.

Medicare, a fundamental healthcare pillar for many seniors, also comes into play. While Medicare Part A is typically covered by the government, Part B comes with a price tag. And guess what? The price you pay is *directly correlated* to your total income. With RMDs bumping up your income, they can and do inadvertently trigger **IRMAA** and hike up the cost of Medicare Part B and Part D as well.

Now, I can almost hear the wheels turning as you're turning the pages, wondering, *What exactly do you mean by tax-deferred accounts?* So, let's break it down.

Fast Fact: *About 40% of people who get Social Security have to pay income taxes on their benefits.*[55]

---

[55] SSA "Social Security Administration: Retirement Benefits" 2023 https://www.ssa.gov/pubs/EN-05-10035.pdf Page 11 Accessed 12/20/2023.

THE 3 WORLDS OF TAXES

There are three worlds of taxes when it comes to your retirement savings. By learning how to keep below certain income thresholds, you can learn how to diversify your retirement income from a tax standpoint to maximize your tax-free income, minimize your RMD, and keep more of your money for you and your family.

THE TAXABLE WORLD

You will pay taxes every year on the money inside taxable accounts.

This income is reported as dividend or interest income on your 1099 tax form. Most people have at least some money in taxable accounts. Examples of these accounts include your savings, money market savings account, bank CDs, individual bonds, individual stocks, and brokerage accounts that are *not* retirement accounts.

The drawback of taxable accounts is that you must pay taxes on any interest earned even if you don't plan to spend the money. For example, if your bank CD earned 2 percent for the year, but you're in a five-year contract, you would still owe taxes on the amount of interest earned before the CD matures. This can eat into your profits, making it difficult to keep up with inflation. If you have too much money in taxable accounts, then you might want to work with a knowledgeable adviser who can help you do tax *planning* rather than simply tax *paying*.

Fast Fact: *49% of retirees reported that their spending was higher than expected, and that included taxes.*[56]

THE TAX-DEFERRED WORLD

You will not have to pay taxes on the money in these accounts *until* you take it out, or when you reach a certain age, and the IRS requires you to withdraw a certain amount.

Tax-deferred accounts are sometimes called qualified accounts. Why? Because they qualify for a certain kind of tax treatment. This deal allows you to save the money *before* the income has been taxed, allowing it to grow tax-deferred until you go to spend it *later*. If you're participating in your company's retirement plan such as 401(k) or Thrift Savings Plan, 403(b), 457, IRA, SEP IRA, Simple IRA, Spousal IRA, or profit-sharing plans, then congratulations, you will qualify for retirement taxes.

These taxes come due when you take this money out. If you don't need the money right away and you keep growing it, you will have to spend it eventually according to the rules. The tax-deferred retirement accounts listed above all have Required Minimum Distributions—known as the RMD—that become due once you reach a certain age.

The age of this RMD has changed twice with the passing of the SECURE Act, first to age 72, and now as of January

---

[56] Retirement Confidence Survey, 2023, EBRI, https://www.ebri.org/docs/default-source/rcs/2023-rcs/2023-rcs-short-report.pdf Page 21, Accessed 1/09/2024.

2023, to age 73.[57] Because of the SECURE Act 2.0, the RMD will eventually become age 75 by the year 2033.[58] This is the age at which you must take this money out, but there's no law that says you can't take it out earlier.

Why would you want to take the money out earlier? Because if this account grows too large, future withdrawals (or even just your RMD obligations) could cause a lot of problems later such as a higher tax rate, a bigger tax bill, a smaller amount of Social Security income, and a hike to your Medicare premiums.

Thankfully, you do have the option of moving this money into a different account where the money can be withdrawn tax-free.

Fast Fact: *Between the ages of 59½ and 73, there is no rule that restricts how much or how little you must take out of your tax-deferred retirement account.*[59]

THE TAX-FREE WORLD

Tax-free accounts give you tax-free income. How delicious is that?

Everybody gets some form of tax-free income during retirement thanks to Social Security. At least 15 percent of

---

[57] Senate Finance Committee, SECURE 2.0 Act of 2022 Title I, Jan 2023, https://www.finance.senate.gov/imo/media/doc/Secure%202.0_Section%20by%20Section%20Summary%2012-19-22%20FINAL.pdf Accessed 1/4/2023.
[58] Ibid.
[59] IRS, When Can a Retirement Plan Distribute Benefits? April 2023, https://www.irs.gov/retirement-plans/plan-participant-employee/when-can-a-retirement-plan-distribute-benefits Accessed 6/21/2023.

this income will be paid to you tax-free, and some people receive all their Social Security income tax-free. How much of your Social Security income will be taxed depends on your *provisional income*, which, if you're curious, you can ask me about. Up to 85 percent of your benefit may be taxed, and it will be taxed at your highest marginal income tax rate.

All Roth IRA accounts give you 100 percent tax-free retirement income. This is because the money is taxed when it's going in, so it won't be taxed again when it's coming out.

Every dollar you take out of a Roth will cost you zero dollars in taxes.

With a Roth, even the gains earned by the money comes to you tax-free, which is why many people like Maureen and her friend Mimi consider doing Roth conversions.

A Roth conversion is when you move the money *out* of a traditional IRA or retirement account and *into* a Roth account. While you first must pay the tax debt owed, and there are rules, every dollar you convert from a traditional IRA into a Roth IRA can come back to you in the form of tax-free retirement income later, and that includes any gains earned.

Here is the cliff-notes version to make this easier to remember:

Taxable accounts = tax me now.
Tax-deferred accounts = tax me later.
Tax-free accounts = tax me never.

We know that tax laws and rates change over time. ***We know what the tax rates are now, but we don't know where they will be in the future.*** All signs point to the probability of rising taxes. The more you can reduce your tax liability now, the less income your portfolio must generate in the future to support your lifestyle—meaning you can assume less risk with the same outcome.

Fast Fact: *Studies find that a more tax-efficient withdrawal strategy can help boost your nest egg anywhere from 1 to 11%.*[60]

THE WINDOW OF TAX OPPORTUNITY

Let's not confuse *paying* your taxes with *planning* for your taxes. Paying your taxes is what you do every year by the deadline of April 15. By then, it's usually too late to do anything but pay what you owe.

Planning for your taxes means looking ahead—sometimes as long as 10 years into the future—and using current tax law to your advantage.

So, looking ahead, how many people think that tax rates will be going *down* during the next 15 years?

Nobody.

How many people think taxes will be going *up*?

Everybody.

---

[60] Geisler, Greg; Harden, Bill; Hulse, David S., A Comparison of the Tax Efficiency of Decumulation Strategies, Financial Planning Association (FPA), March 2021, https://www.financialplanningassociation.org/article/journal/MAR21-comparison-tax-efficiency-decumulation-strategies Accessed 12/05/2023.

When you think about retirement spanning 20 to 30 years, and you look at where we are today as compared to where we've been, it becomes pretty obvious which direction we're headed. The question is, how high will they go?

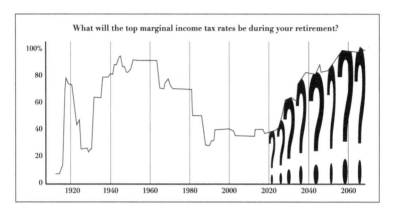

Source: Magellan Finanical using data from the Urban-Brookings Tax Policy Center, "Historical Individual Income Tax Parameters.' 1913 to 2016."

On November 16, 2017, the House of Representatives passed the Tax Cuts and Jobs Act to reform the individual income tax codes. This act lowered tax rates on wages, investment, and business income, and it changed the standard deductions for millions of filers, nearly doubling the standard amount. But these individual income-tax changes are set to expire on December 31, 2025, when tax brackets will revert to 2017 levels.[61] This will be a significant day for most taxpayers.

---

[61] El-Sibaie, Amir, A Look Ahead at Expiring Tax Provisions, Tax Foundation, https://taxfoundation.org/look-ahead-expiring-tax-provisions Accessed 6/23/2023.

Twenty-three provisions are set to expire, so most taxpayers will see a tax hike unless provisions are extended.[62]

What this means for you is that right now we have a window of opportunity where it's possible to do some real planning. Taxes are at historically low levels. They aren't going to stay this low forever.

Fast Fact: *The highest marginal tax rate ever seen was 94% in 1944-1945. It remained in the 50% to 90% range until it went down in 1987 to 38.50%.*[63]

TAKE THE REINS FROM THE IRS

Retirement accounts have rules about when and how much money you may put in. Some of these accounts also have rules about when and how much you must take out. Take the traditional IRA. The rules look like this:

- Contributions you make are tax-deferred.
- The growth inside the IRA? That's tax-deferred as well.
- If you decide to withdraw before age 59 ½, there's a 10 percent penalty awaiting.
- When you do make withdrawals, the taxman comes knocking. Taxes are owed on all those amounts.
- These accounts come with the pesky RMD we talked about.

---

[62] Ibid.
[63] Tax Policy Center, Historical Highest Marginal Income Tax Rates, May 2023, https://www.taxpolicycenter.org/statistics/historical-highest-marginal-income-tax-rates Accessed 6/23/2023.

Speaking of the RMD—how much will you have to take out? To calculate the exact amount of your RMD, the IRS uses a division formula based on two things:
1) Your account's balance at the end of the preceding year.
2) The number of years that you're expected to live.

Your RMD amount is then calculated by dividing your tax-deferred retirement account balance as of December 31 of last year by your life expectancy factor.

The IRS calculates your life expectancy by looking at the Uniform Lifetime Table. This table calculates the number of years that you have left to pay the taxes you owe on this amount of money. The longer you live, the more the account grows, and the shorter amount of time you have left to pay the taxes owed.

Mathematically speaking, if you're dividing a number that keeps getting bigger by a number that keeps getting lower, **the amount of your RMD will keep getting higher**. As you get older and need this money less, you'll be required to take out more money from an account that you'd potentially intended to leave for someone else, meanwhile triggering those ugly tax consequences.

FOR USE BY IRA OWNERS IN 2022 AND BEYOND

Uniform Lifetime Table			Uniform Lifetime Table		
Age	Life Expectancy Factor	RMD% Equivalent	Age	Life Expectancy Factor	RMD% Equivalent
72	27.4	3.65%	97	7.8	12.82%
73	26.5	3.77%	98	7.3	13.70%
74	25.5	3.92%	99	6.8	14.71%
75	24.6	4.07%	100	6.4	15.63%
76	23.7	4.22%	101	6	16.67%
77	22.9	4.37%	102	5.6	17.86%
78	22	4.55%	103	5.2	19.23%
79	21.1	4.74%	104	4.9	20.41%
80	20.2	4.95%	105	4.6	21.74%
81	19.4	5.15%	106	4.3	23.26%
82	18.5	5.41%	107	4.1	24.39%
83	17.7	5.65%	108	3.9	25.64%
84	16.8	5.95%	109	3.7	27.03%
85	16	6.25%	110	3.5	28.57%
86	15.2	6.58%	111	3.4	29.41%
87	14.4	6.94%	112	3.3	30.30%
88	13.7	7.30%	113	3.1	32.26%
89	12.9	7.75%	114	3	33.33%
90	12.2	8.20%	115	2.9	34.48%
91	11.5	8.70%	116	2.8	35.71%
92	10.8	9.26%	117	2.7	37.04%
93	10.1	9.90%	118	2.5	40.00%
94	9.5	10.53%	119	2.3	43.48%
95	8.9	11.24%	120	2	50.00%
96	8.4	11.90%			

The Roth IRA is different. How different? I'm so glad you asked.

The key advantage I want you to grasp when you think about converting is that by making this strategic move now, you're essentially taking the reins from the IRS and deciding for yourself when and how you'll the tackle taxes owed on your retirement savings.

Imagine a scenario where you've deferred taxes on your savings for 50 years. Now, in your mid-70s, the IRS comes knocking, forcing you to withdraw and pay up through those pesky RMDs. It's like being on a financial timer you didn't set!

With the Roth conversion, you sidestep this whole ordeal. You're saying, "I'll pay the taxes now, so I can enjoy my money, on my terms, later." It's all about being proactive and regaining control. The power to decide is back in your hands, not with the IRS.

Let's compare. With a Roth, the tax situation looks like this:

- You pay taxes upfront, at the time of your contribution.
- Here's the sweet part – all growth inside the Roth? Absolutely tax-free.
- Now, it is an IRA. So, if you're tempted to withdraw before age 59 ½, you're still looking at that 10 percent penalty.
- Once you start withdrawing *post* 59 ½, it's like the taxman doesn't exist for this account—withdrawals are tax-free.
- And, say goodbye to RMDs! Roth IRAs are NOT subject to them.
- If all that sounds good to you, let's get into the nitty-gritty of Roth IRAs. How do you get one? What's the trick when trying to convert? Let's focus on the rules.

Fast Fact: *Once your RMD becomes due, for every dollar you fail to withdraw the IRS will charge a 25% penalty.*[64]

---

[64] IRS, Retirement Plan and IRA Required Minimum Distributions FAQs, March 2023, https://www.irs.gov/retirement-plans/retirement-plan-and-ira-required-minimum-distributions-faqs#:~:text=the%20required%20deadline%3F-,(updated%20March%2014%2C%20 2023),timely%20corrected%20within%20two%20years Access 5/5/2023.

RULES OF THE ROTH

First and foremost, to contribute to a Roth IRA, you need to have what's called *earned income*. This is income you receive in exchange for your time and effort—think wages or salaries.

Social Security? Nope.
Pension payments? Nope.
Distributions from tax-deferred accounts? Also no.
Dividends and rental incomes? Not considered earned income either.

So, this is wildly important: If you don't have earned income, you can't contribute to a Roth IRA. (But don't stop reading—*contributing* is different from *converting*!)

Now, suppose you've checked that box and have earned income. Great! But here's the catch: If you're earning *too much* income, you can't contribute to a Roth IRA. Yup. For 2024, if you're filing taxes as a single individual, you should be making less than $161,000 to be eligible.[65] Married folks? Keep that **combined income** under $240,000.[66]

So, you've got earned income, you're under the threshold—what's next? How much can you put in? Well, for 2024, if you're under age 50, you can contribute up to $7,000. Over age 50? That goes up to $8,000.[67] Compare this to 401(k)s where the limits are $23,000 and $30,500 respectively.[68] So yes, Roth contribution limits are a tad

---

[65] IRS, 401(k) limit increases to $23,000 for 2024, IRA limit rises to $7,000, Nov 2023, https://www.irs.gov/newsroom/401k-limit-increases-to-23000-for-2024-ira-limit-rises-to-7000 Accessed 1/10/2024.
[66] Ibid.
[67] Ibid.
[68] Ibid.

restrictive. But keep in mind, the magic with the Roth is in the tax-free withdrawals. And if you're smart and wait until after 59 ½, you also dodge that 10 percent penalty.

Now, for all you folks who are retired or are about to become retired and unemployed—here's a neat trick if these contribution rules seem a bit constraining:

Instead of contributing, consider converting!

Convert funds from a traditional IRA to a Roth IRA. Yes, you'll pay taxes during the conversion, but any growth after that? Completely tax-free. And the beauty of conversions? No earned income requirement, no income ceilings, and no limit to the conversion amount.

However, be strategic with this. You don't want your current tax bill to skyrocket and negate the benefits of future tax-free growth. Using the marginal income tax rates as a guide and working with an advisor, it's possible to pull out a strategic amount from your IRA every year while staying below your income threshold to fund a Roth. These withdrawals will be taxed as income at your current rate because a Roth is funded with post-tax money. But because Roth withdrawals are not taxed later, even on the interest they accumulate, it can be a better deal for someone in a rising-tax environment.

Roth conversions are not for everyone. They require proper tax planning and an advisor who takes a holistic approach because conversions could trigger unintended tax consequences if they are not carefully analyzed. In some cases, consulting with multiple professionals might be appropriate. They'll be able to work out the math so see

if it's worth it. When you convert to a Roth, you receive significant tax advantages:
- No RMDs.
- Tax-free growth.
- Tax-free income.
- Tax-free money to your beneficiaries.

One of the most powerful and often overlooked features of the Roth IRA is how it benefits your heirs. Up next: Let's talk about what happens when you have assets to leave behind.

Fast Fact: *After the passage of the SECURE Act, the new 10-year requirement for non-spousal inherited IRAs is forecast to generate $15.75 billion in federal revenues from 2020 through 2029.*[69]

WHAT ABOUT YOUR FAMILY?

With most tax-deferred accounts like traditional IRAs or 401(k)s, your beneficiaries will face a tax bill when they inherit. Why? Because these taxes have been deferred and not paid. Before the passing of the SECURE Act, beneficiaries who inherited were allowed to s-t-r-e-t-c-h out their distributions and the associated tax bills over *their* lifetimes. However, with the passage of the Secure Act, that option is off the table.

---

[69] Prescott, Gregory L., Hardin, James R., Rich, James C., The Secure Act Ushers in Sweeping Retirement Plan Changes, CPA Journal, April 2021 https://www.cpajournal.com/2021/06/23/the-secure-act-ushers-in-sweeping-retirement-plan-changes/ Accessed 12/5/2023.

Signed into law in 2019, the SECURE Act gives your beneficiaries just 10 years to settle up with the IRS. If they decide to spend their inheritance even quicker, they might find themselves with an even bigger tax bill.

What does this mean to your family?

Imagine for a minute that your granddaughter has just entered her accumulation years. She's single and is earning a salary of, say, $50,000 annually. Then, she inherits her father's $500,000 IRA.

What's going to happen?

If she does the smart thing and rolls it over into an *inherited IRA*, she won't owe the taxes all at once. She will, however, owe them in 10 years. If she divides the amount by 10 to pay them gradually, she will withdraw roughly 10 percent of the account value, or $50,000 annually. This amount would be added to her income total, throwing her into a *much* higher tax bracket than what she was currently paying. If she chooses to spend this money all at once, the taxes would be even worse.

If you didn't save this money so that Uncle Sam could be one of your biggest inheritors, then a Roth stands out as a beacon of hope. When you leave a Roth IRA to your heirs, they can inherit it tax-free. This is also true for your surviving spouse. They're free to use this money as they see fit, without constantly looking over their shoulder for the taxman.

Fast Fact: *Studies find that 40% of wealthy households—defined as having a combined income from Social Security and savings averaging $7,242 a month—are at risk of not being able to maintain their lifestyle due to taxation.*[70]

It doesn't take a whole lot of brains to look at your portfolio only in terms of the rate of return and how much it can *earn*. The real test is understanding how to think like a tax planner by looking at your portfolio in terms of **how much money you get to *keep*.**

At Quest, we're not afraid to recommend *and* provide a CPA, a lawyer, or a Medicare specialist—whatever it is you need to get this planning done right. There are a lot of traps and pitfalls that even the smartest among us can fall into. That's why we recommend working with a team of advisers when putting advanced strategies like a Roth conversion in place.

---

[70] Chen, Anqi, and Munnell, Alicia H., How Much Taxes Will Retirees Owe On Their Retirement Income? Center for Retirement Research at Boston College, November 2020, Page 15, https://crr.bc.edu/wp-content/uploads/2020/11/wp_2020-16..pdf Accessed 5/04/2023.

CHANGE YOUR MINDSET: NEXT STEPS

LOOK AT YOUR ESTATE IN TERMS OF HOW MUCH MONEY YOU GET TO KEEP.

- Consider state taxes on your income. Some places have more favorable tax rates on retirement income than others. Eight states have no income tax whatsoever—not even on Social Security income—while nine states offer no taxes on retirement distributions, including pension income.[71]
- What are the property taxes where you live? In 2023, New Jersey has the highest property tax rate at 2.47 percent, followed by Illinois, New Hampshire, and Connecticut, all above 2 percent.[72] Consider a 2 percent drain over the course of a 30-year retirement, and choose a retirement residence based on how much of your money you can *keep*.
- Assess the assets you own that have increased in value, such as your home, art, or stocks. If the value is worth more than what it was when purchased, how can you protect these assets from Medicaid spend-down? When is the best time to sell—before, or after you die?

---

[71] Washington, Katelyn, States That Tax Social Security Benefits in 2024, Kiplinger, February 2024, https://www.kiplinger.com/retirement/social-security/603803/states-that-tax-social-security-benefits Accessed 2/15/2024.
[72] World Population View, Property Taxes by State, 2023, https://worldpopulationreview.com/state-rankings/property-taxes-by-state Accessed 12/29/2023.

- Update your beneficiary designations to include marriage, recent births, and death. If you don't want your ex to inherit your 401(k), just putting that in a **will** won't be good enough if their name is still listed on your retirement account.
- If you are still working, open a Roth IRA account and get that five-year clock ticking. All interest earned, whether from dividends or capital gains, is distributed tax-free on deposits that are at least five years old.

STEP 6

BREAK UP WITH YOUR CURRENT ADVISER

"The rare individual who unselfishly tries to serve others has an enormous advantage."

~Dale Carnegie

The longer you live, the longer you are likely to keep on living, and this was true for Shirley, a proud homeowner in the city of Detroit. Shirley was one of the original women who started it all. She and her cohorts were working with our CEO Gene Wittstock years before the Great Recession of 2008. Way back in the 1990s, Gene had set Shirley up in an investment plan that would see her *to* and *through* retirement. Every year, our firm reviewed that plan.

One year, after Shirley had retired and entered her early 70s, we were reviewing her plan when she told us, "I want to pay for my granddaughter's college."

We listened while she explained why this was so important to her. This granddaughter had received a scholarship to a prestigious university, but it didn't cover everything. Shirley had vowed to become this young woman's benefactor and see to it that she got the education she deserved.

"This is non-negotiable," she explained. "I will eat ramen noodles, if I must, although I'd rather not. What do the numbers tell you?"

According to our lifespan calculator, given Shirley's age and healthy habits, she would likely go on living to the age of 105. While this was exciting news, it also meant we needed to adjust her plan to accommodate the withdrawals for her granddaughter's college tuition.

"We will need to reduce your monthly expenses by $200 a month," I explained after doing the math. "I know that's a lot, but we have a team of advisers here who can help you."

Now, nobody wants to hear that they have to reduce their expenses in retirement. The first place we always look is homeowner and car insurance, which tends to be high for people who live in the city of Detroit. A lot of times with property and casualty, they reduce your coverage or increase your deductible, meaning your payments go up every five to six years.

"We have somebody here who specializes in this," I explained, "and a lot of times, he's able to get you the exact same or even better coverage for less money."

In our office here at Quest, we have an insurance expert named Wayne who came on board with us a few years ago after he shut his own practice down. Having spent a career in insurance services, Wayne had retired, but he missed the interactions with his clients. He kept his license active, and so we asked him, "Why not come in a couple of days a week and help our clients out?" We struck up an agreement that worked for both of us, Wayne came on board, and our team was made stronger because of it.

His assessment of Shirley's situation surprised us.

"The problem is her credit score," Wayne said when it came time to share his findings. "I can get a much better insurance rate for the exact same coverage, but first, Shirley, you have to get your credit score up by 30 points."

Shirley laughed. "I own my house and my own car," she said. "What do I care about my credit score?!"

"It's the insurance company that cares," Wayne explained. "They will punish you with higher rates if it's not as high as they'd like to see it."

Shirley looked glum.

"Hey, don't worry," I said. "We can help you with this. In fact, I'm the perfect person to help because there was a time in my life when I had destroyed my credit. So, this is what we will do: I'll take you through a little program, and we will help you build your credit score."

Shirley was game, and so that's what we did. She went through the program and was amazed to see her score rise by 30 points. A few months later, we set up another meeting with Wayne.

Now, Wayne redid her homeowner's insurance based on the new credit score, and he was able to get her the *exact same coverage* for $230 fewer dollars a month.

"That's $30 more than I had before," she exclaimed. "Now, I can treat all the grandkids to ice cream every month!"

We had found a way to cut $200 from her monthly budget—without sacrificing coverage or changing her retirement. We didn't make any money off this transaction, but now, we knew that Shirley could help her granddaughter and not run out of money even if she lived to age 105.

Later, after Shirley left, I thanked Wayne for helping us out. That was when I learned how he had gone above and beyond.

Earlier before our meeting, when he had punched in the exact street address for Shirley's home, the insurance company changed the rate on him. They hiked it up, and so he called them to find out why.

"She lives in a neighborhood with too many vacant properties," they explained. "We can't take the risk."

So, what did Wayne do?

He got in his car and drove out to the neighborhood where Shirley lived. He took pictures to show the insurance company that she lived on a good street and took care of her house. Shirley had kept up with the painting, maintenance, and repairs; she'd even planted a garden and put in a new front walkway. When he sent those pictures to the insurance company, they said, "Okay," and he got her the better rate.[73]

This is a story based on a true situation and why I am so proud to be a member of the Quest team. The financial services industry is supposed to be all about serving. Serving is not a transactional business; it's a relationship

---

[73] Based on a true story using fictional characters with actual figures from sources believed to be reliable. This example is shown for illustrative purposes only. Your results may vary.

one! A lot of people haven't had the opportunity to experience true planning help in this way.

Because retirement planning has gotten more complicated than it used to be, more is being asked of you. In return, you might also expect more from your adviser.

- Are they talking to you about budgetary concerns, homeowner's insurance, market risk, and taxes?
- Can they help you with your Medicare decisions?
- Can they get you an income stream that will take you all the way through retirement?
- Can they give you a written plan where it tells you in black and white *when* you can retire and *how much* income you will receive?
- Can this income be guaranteed?
- Is this plan flexible?

While the title of this chapter is meant to be somewhat facetious, there is truth to it, because research finds that who you work with matters. By taking the time to consider all the factors that can impact your happiness in retirement, including both financial and non-financial matters, your nest egg will stand a better chance of supporting the kind of retirement that you've envisioned.

If you are approaching or in retirement, then you want to work with an independent, fiduciary adviser who specializes in the distribution of your assets so you can get a true plan. This chapter is here to help you ask all the right questions to get what you need.

Fast Fact: *Your choice of a financial adviser can dramatically affect your retirement savings due to variations in fees, compensation, and conflicts of interest.*[74]

GET ADVICE THAT IS FOR *YOU*

The other day I had someone come into my office asking about a video for a financial strategy he had seen online.

"Should I do this?" he said. "I get this monthly newsletter from this guy, and he made this 'chasing the alpha' thing sound really great."

"Listen," I told him. "It might be really great, but 99 percent of the financial news you hear and read about online is not for you."

It's not for you! On the internet, television, radio—they are not talking to you. They are talking to people who have 30 to 50 years left on their time horizon, and so because they don't need this money, they are willing to take a risk for the potential of a gain. Buy this, buy that, oil stocks, bitcoin, cryptocurrency—it's not for you!

Once you've saved the money for retirement, you've already won the game. It's time to quit playing, take the chips off the table, and take steps to prepare what you've earned so that it can provide for your future. If you've come all the way through this book with me, then you know that the management of your funds in retirement is totally

---

[74] The Pew Charitable Trusts, Issue Brief: Choice of Financial Adviser Can Dramatically Affect Retirement Savings, July 2022 https://www.pewtrusts.org/en/research-and-analysis/issue-briefs/2022/07/choice-of-financial-adviser-can-dramatically-affect-retirement-savings Accessed 12/17/2023.

different than the management of your funds during your working years.

Living off your nest egg is different than building a nest egg.

You might have had a financial professional who led you here down the yellow brick road to this point in your life. Great! You made it to Oz! The Promised Land!

Now, you need to do something different in order to make this money last.

Nine out of ten times, the person who got you here isn't equipped to manage your distributions effectively. In today's world of online advice, you've probably come across different terms for financial professionals and seen the term "advisor" spelled with an "o". In this book, we have been very intentional about our spelling of "adviser" with an "e" because of the laws that govern investment adviser representatives. I am an investment adviser representative held to the fiduciary standard, not to be confused with registered financial professionals, or broker dealers. These two types of investment professionals are not the same:

- An *investment adviser* is an individual or company who provides advice about investments to their clients. They are held to the fiduciary "best interest of the client" standard.
- Registered financial professionals are licensed sales personnel, known as brokers, who work for broker-dealer firms to buy and sell investments. They are held to a standard dictated by the *suitability rule*.

Both broker dealers and investment advisers can be referred to as "financial advisors." They can both buy and sell stocks and other market investments on your behalf. Ironically, all or most of the bulleted persons below can also refer to themselves as 'advisors' or even "financial advisers" even though they may not have the proper licensing or training. This can make it difficult to know who you are working with.

- Insurance-only agents can get you access to income vehicles such as fixed annuities in the *Protected World* but *not* investments or stocks from the *Potential World*. Therefore, they are not legally considered investment advisers or registered financial professionals.
- Broker-dealers can give you access to the *Potential World* of stocks and bonds, but typically not vehicles from the *Hybrid World* such as the fixed-indexed annuity. Therefore, they may not specialize in the distribution phase of life.
- Independent investment advisers who have their insurance license—or those who work alongside a team of licensed professionals like myself—can give you access to a full spectrum of investments from all *Three Worlds of Money*, including *Protected*, *Potential*, and *Hybrid*. They can help you plan for all three financial phases: accumulation, preservation, and distribution.
- An investment adviser representative is held to the fiduciary standard and legally required to give you advice that is in your best interest. A registered investment advisory firm, known as RIA, is also held to the same fiduciary standards.

Fast Fact: *The fiduciary duty comprises of a duty of care and loyalty, which applies to the entire relationship between the adviser and client.*[75]

THE BROKER VS. THE FIDUCIARY

Advisers who buy and sell investments from the *Potential World* are held to ethical standards that can be enforced by law. The key thing to realize here is that not all advisors focus on retirement planning. Some of them are better suited to helping you get *to* retirement rather than *through* it. As such, the assets and money worlds they have access to will reflect that. As someone coming from the other side of the table, having just gone through the process of looking for an adviser, I think the biggest difference is the standard of care these professionals are held to.

It's easy for someone to talk about losing money when the money isn't theirs. Whether the market goes up, down, or sideways, the broker still gets his commission fee. A broker is also held to a different standard of accountability known as the "suitability rule."

Recently in 2020, the suitability rule was changed to include an investor's age, tax status, and liquidity needs—among other things. These are all the things that we as fiduciaries *always* consider when putting together complete and true retirement plans. But for the broker dealer, this standard was new. FINRA Rule 2111,

---

[75] Clayton, Jay, Regulation Best Interest and the Investment Adviser Fiduciary Duty: Two Strong Standards that Protect and Provide Choice for Main Street Investors, U.S. Securities and Exchange Commission, updated April 2023, https://www.sec.gov/tm/standards-conduct-broker-dealers-and-investment-advisers Accessed 1/16/2024.

as it is known, basically says that to comply with the suitability rule, the advisor must do the best they can, and if they make a mistake, either due to ignorance or misunderstanding—oopsie—it's okay, because the product can still be said to be suitable for *some* investors.

This comes down to a question of the captive versus the independent agent. This is why our CEO Gene Wittstock elected to go independent. He left the brokerage firm where he was working when he realized he could not properly serve his clients under these standards.

The regulatory authority FINRA puts it this way:

"Reasonable-basis suitability has two main components: a broker must (1) perform reasonable diligence to understand the potential risks and rewards associated with a recommended security or strategy and (2) determine whether the recommendation is suitable for at least *some* investors based on that understanding. **A broker can violate reasonable-basis suitability** under either prong of the test. That is, even if a firm's product committee has approved a product for sale, an individual broker's **lack of understanding of a recommended product or strategy could violate the obligation**, notwithstanding that the recommendation is suitable for some investors."[76]

---

[76] FINRA, FINRA Rule 2111 (Suitability) FAQ, https://www.finra.org/rules-guidance/key-topics/suitability/faq Accessed 1/10/2024.

Fast Fact: *Many investors are unaware of or confused about various fees they may pay for investing and 38% of mutual fund owners believe— incorrectly—that they do not pay any fees.*[77]

CONTINUE THE QUEST

At Quest Commonwealth, formerly known as Quest Financial, I am privileged to work alongside a team of fiduciary professionals who make it their business to specialize in areas that I do not. Because they have been handpicked by our firm, I know they will go the extra mile when taking care of our clients. Because we are independent, we are not limited by brand, bank, or company when doing this. We can get you access to virtually any product from the Three Worlds of Money: *Protected, Potential,* or *Hybrid.*

We can do this because, as a collective, we have the training and licenses to do so. Furthermore, we do all this while holding ourselves to the highest standard in the industry: the fiduciary standard.

The fiduciary comprises of a duty of care, trust, and loyalty that requires an adviser to serve in the best interest of the client at all times.[78] *That includes a full disclosure of all fees.* If there are financial products or solutions that

---

[77] Investors in the United States: The Changing Landscape, A Report of the FINRA Foundation National Financial Capability Study, December 2022, https://finrafoundation.org/sites/finra-foundation/files/NFCS-Investor-Report-Changing-Landscape.pdf Accessed 1/11/2024
[78] Peirce, Hester M., Outsourcing Fiduciary Duty to the Commission: Statement on Proposed Outsourcing by Investment Advisers, Securities and Exchange Commission, October 2022, https://www.sec.gov/news/statement/peirce-service-providers-oversight-102622 Accessed 1/10/2024.

will better serve you, a fiduciary must eliminate or disclose all conflicts of interest which might cause the adviser—consciously or unconsciously—to give advice that is not in your best interest. A fiduciary is also required to base their advice *not* on commission fees but on the client's objectives. This is why fiduciaries begin *not* with the numbers but with a series of questions designed *to get to know you.*

In our initial meeting, we aim to develop a comprehensive understanding of who you are—your needs, your goals, and the concerns that keep you awake at night. We'll also gauge your appetite for risk to ensure we're aligned in our approach. Likewise, you'll have the opportunity to learn about us—our mission, the services we offer, and how we tackle the issues that weigh most heavily on your mind. We'll also discuss what you can expect from us going forward and address any questions you may have. If our services align with what you're seeking, then you may choose to take advantage of our complimentary retirement analysis. In that case, we'll set up a follow-up meeting to delve into the financial details.

Generally speaking, fiduciaries are more concerned with getting to know the person and establishing a relationship of trust rather than selling you a certain product or investment. If retirement income is one of your worries, then they'll be able to recommend a combination of products from the *Three Worlds of Money* that can get you a regular, recurring income stream if that's what you need. They will also take the time to alert you to all the risks you could face given today's elongated retirement time.

If your advisor is not able to help you coordinate all these things, then it's likely that they do not specialize in helping someone get all the way *through* retirement.

Fast Fact: *It's difficult for consumers to find objective financial information because the industry spends over 400 times more on marketing dollars than federal agencies spend on basic financial education.*[79]

Getting your retirement planning right isn't just a matter of financial security; it's a matter of fulfilling the dreams and aspirations you've worked so hard for. The first few years of retirement are particularly critical, often referred to as the *Red Zone*, where financial missteps can and do have long-lasting repercussions. Remember the math of account value restoration? Remember the sequence of returns? This is a time when your retirement savings are most vulnerable, especially if you encounter market downturns while also drawing an income from your portfolio.

Making the right decisions during this *Red Zone* period can set the stage for a comfortable, worry-free retirement. By strategically allocating your investments across the *Three Worlds of Money—Potential, Protection*, and *Hybrid*—you not only safeguard your nest egg but also give

---

[79] Consumer Financial Protection Bureau, Financial Literacy Report, March 2022, https://files.consumerfinance.gov/f/documents/cfpb_financial-literacy-fy-2021_annual-report_2022-03.pdf Accessed 6/30/2023.

yourself the flexibility and peace of mind to truly enjoy your golden years.

Don't leave your life's work to chance; ensure you have a well-balanced portfolio that aligns with your retirement objectives.

CHANGE YOUR MINDSET: NEXT STEPS

EVALUATE YOUR CURRENT ADVISOR: THE FIVE ESSENTIAL QUESTIONS.

- What ethical and legal standard are you held to?
- Are you an independent adviser?
- Can you show me a written report that discloses all the fees I am paying to you?
- Can you guarantee my retirement income? If yes, how much will it cost me?
- Can you give me a written retirement plan that shows me how much money I will have moving forward for the rest of my life?

EPILOGUE

"Let a man radically alter his thoughts, and he will be astonished at the rapid transformation it will affect in the material conditions of his life."

~ James Allen

From the beginning, you have watched me learn how to figure out retirement. When my wife Medina lost her job, we were looking at my job and her severance package and wondering what to do. We met with the big corporations who set us up with the free call and a questionnaire; we looked at the robo-plans, the big banks, and the one-man shops. We learned how to ask about customer service (can you get a real person to answer the phone?) and successions plans (if you're with a one-man firm, and something happens to them, who takes over the management of the plan?). We took the meetings and made the calls, and we were just not finding what we needed and deserved.

Then, we met Gene Wittstock at Quest Commonwealth, and everything clicked. Once he threw the *Three Worlds of Money* in front of me, I knew I had found my guy. Nothing he did was robotic. Everything he did was real. My wife and I were actual people to him, and he wanted to do right by us. This was what I had been looking for, and from that first meeting, I knew: balancing our portfolio among the *Three Worlds of Money* would get us both *to* and *through* retirement.

Everything Gene taught me, I have put in this book. My wife Medina is now retired from her job with AT&T, and if she works, it's because she wants to—at a yoga studio, volunteering her time. I am working as one of the fiduciary investment advisers at Quest Commonwealth, the firm where we finally found the answers to our questions and got a true plan in place. I say "work," but really, it is a true privilege to serve the men and women who come physically and virtually through our doors.

As we conclude this journey through the *Safe Money Mindset*, I'd like you to pause and reflect on the essence of achieving a retirement that aligns with your dreams and goals. The key difference between those who merely *hope* for a secure retirement and those who *actually attain it* boils down to one crucial factor: Mindset.

It's the individuals who successfully shift their mindset—from mere accumulation to preservation and distribution, from ignoring risk to managing it, and from one-dimensional investing to a balanced approach across the *Three Worlds of Money*—who navigate the complexities of retirement successfully. If you're ready to make this mindset shift and truly prioritize your future, we invite you to reach out for a complimentary, comprehensive retirement analysis tailored for you today.

If you're not comfortable with this idea, if you're just not jiving with the information presented here, then you are free to go on your way. I am not going to beg or chase you down the street. When I ask someone out to prom, and they say, "No, thanks," I'm not the guy who stands out on the lawn with a boombox over my head playing "In Your Eyes." I respect your decision and move on. We recognize a client's freedom of choice; we value self-worth and protect it as our own. I want this relationship to be beneficial for both of us.

So, I won't serenade you; but I do hope you have learned a few things. Learning is time consuming. The only way to grow is to fail, and that can take years. I've had the privilege of learning from an expert with proven success—Gene Wittstock has given me the benefit of decades of experience in just a short amount of time. I have put all these lessons into this book so that you don't have to go through the pain of failure. Whether you work with us or someone else, all I ask is that you don't leave your hard-earned life's work to chance; take the step to embrace the *Safe Money Mindset* and get a true and comprehensive plan in place.

CHANGE YOUR MINDSET: NEXT STEPS
GET A PLAN.

- Contact us for a complimentary, no-obligation portfolio review at 1-866-QUEST-01.
- For Michigan residents, call 248-599-1000.
- Visit us at 30700 Telegraph Rd, Ste 1475, Bingham Farms, MI, 48025.

ABOUT THE AUTHOR

Jeff Perry is an investment adviser representative, co-host of the television show *Safe Money Mindset*, and Chief Marketing Officer serving as Co-Owner at Quest Commonwealth.

As an adviser, Jeff is passionate about leveraging his background to serve the public in the financial domain, providing tailored, one-on-one retirement solutions for clients of any caliber and size. No person's need for quality financial advice is too small or too complex, and all options are on the table. He advocates for a *Safe Money Mindset* and designs financial plans that are stable, inflation resistant, and supportive of the lifestyle you want to live. He does this by integrating the *Three Worlds of Money* that serve as guiding principles for his approach.

Before joining Quest, Jeff served for a decade in the U.S. Navy and then embarked on a 12-year career in advertising. In 2018, Jeff left a lucrative position after his wife, Medina, was surplussed from her position with AT&T. Frustrated after meeting with countless advisors and just not getting the kind of plan he knew they would need, Jeff and his wife set up an appointment with the CEO of Quest. After meeting Gene Wittstock and learning about the *Three Worlds of Money*, not only did Jeff get a true and balanced financial plan, but he also changed his career.

Today, Jeff serves residents in and around Michigan to help them create lasting wealth. During virtual meetings with Jeff, you might also notice several guitars hanging on his wall because, as a musician who sings and writes songs, playing guitar is what helps him to focus and problem solve. When not advising clients, he can be found mentoring veterans as they transition into civilian life, wearing pink as an ambassador for the American Cancer Society, or helping at the SASHA Farm Sanctuary and Safe Haven for neglected animals. Both Jeff and his wife Medina share a love of animals. Together with their daughter they house two cats and multiple dogs.

GENE WITTSTOCK

Gene Wittsock is the Founder and current President of Quest Commonwealth, a full-service, independent firm serving residents of Michigan and beyond.

As a retirement planning specialist with over 25 years of experience, Gene has had the great pleasure of extending his services to a diverse pool of employees across a wide range of industries, including AT&T, Ford, and General Motors. An independent professional by choice, he has worked extensively with mutual funds, annuities, pensions, and other financial tools related to both wealth-building and retirement planning. Throughout his career he has also been a sought-after public speaker, delivering speeches and seminars to countless individuals seeking knowledge about their investment options and the steps they need to take to enjoy a retirement stress-free.

Gene left his home country of Poland due to opposing political beliefs, seeking opportunity in Detroit, Michigan. With only twenty dollars in his pocket and a passion to engage in the city's rich culture, he began work as a laborer to pay his way through college. He went on to earn a Master of Science degree in Finance and Financial Management Services from Walsh College after first completing his bachelor's degree from William Tyndale College.

In the spring of 1997, Gene began his career as a financial advisor at Waddell & Reed before becoming a licensed investment adviser with New England Financial. After witnessing how critical it was to preserve the wealth of his clients during the financial crisis of 2000, Gene left the firm to pursue independence. He discovered an open marketplace that offered a wider array of alternative investments, which was more advantageous to his clients. In 2001, he set up his own agency with a focus on safe money products and developed his client-centric methods focused on transparency, principles, and a moral code of ethics. Over the years, this agency evolved from Wittstock Financial and Associates to Quest Financial, reflecting the importance of holistic planning. In 2022, committed to deeper client engagement and community involvement, he transformed his company yet again to Quest Commonwealth, where he leads the charge today as a defender of wealth.

GLOSSARY OF TERMS

ACCOUNT VALUE RESTORATION – The break-even math that shows how much of a gain you will need to get back to where you were once your account experiences loss.

ACCUMULATION PHASE – The financial phase during your working years when you are saving and growing your assets.

ACTIVE STRATEGY – The ongoing buying and selling of investments based on their short-term performance with the goal of limiting loss in exchange for a portion of the gains.

ANNUITY – An insurance contract where you exchange a lump-sum payment or series of payments in return for a regular income that begins either immediately or at some future date.

BENEFICIARY – An individual entitled to collect assets as decreed by a written, legal document.

BUY-AND-HOLD STRATEGY – A passive investment strategy whereby market investments are bought and then held for a long period regardless of market fluctuations, so investors capture 100 percent of market gains and 100 percent of market loss.

COMBINED INCOME – Also known as your provisional income, the IRS defines combined income as your adjusted gross income, plus tax-exempt interest, plus half of your Social Security benefits.

COMMON STOCKS – A market investment that profits from the future success of a business entity and gives shareholders voting rights.

CORRELATION – The relationship between two things within the realm of investing: if two things are highly correlated, they are moving in the same direction at the same time; if they are inversely correlated, they are moving in opposite directions at the same time.

COST-OF-LIVING-ADJUSTMENT (COLA) – Adjustments that give claimants of Social Security a way to keep pace with inflation and the rising price of goods and services.

DISTRIBUTION PHASE – The financial phase during your non-working years when you shift from saving to spending the assets.

DEFERRED ANNUITY – An annuity that promises to pay the owner a regular income, either as a lump sum or as a lifetime stream, at some future date.

DOLLAR-COST AVERAGING – An investment strategy practiced during your accumulation years where the same amount of money is invested on a regular basis regardless of market performance.

ESTATE PLANNING – The process of transferring your belongings to someone else, including the transfer of assets, obligations, or responsibilities.

FIDUCIARY – A professional who holds a legal or ethical relationship of trust to prudently take care of money or other assets for another person.

INCOME GAP – The difference between your retirement living expenses and the income from guaranteed sources such as pensions or Social Security.

INFLATION RISK – The risk that rising prices associated with the cost of goods and services could outpace the returns delivered by your investments.

IRMAA – An acronym for Medicare's Income-Related Monthly Adjustment Amount, which can charge a higher premium for Medicare Parts B and D for individuals with higher incomes.

LIQUIDITY – How quickly or easily you can convert an asset into cash.

PASSIVE STRATEGY – A long-term investment strategy for building wealth whereby savers purchase investments and hold them without seeking to profit from short-term price fluctuations or market timing.

PRESERVATION PHASE – The financial phase three to five years before retirement when you shift from a growth mindset to one of preservation of your assets.

PRINCIPAL – The base amount of money that you put into an investment.

PROBATE – The legal process by which the assets of the deceased are properly distributed, the objective being to ensure that the deceased's debts, taxes, and other valid claims are paid out of their estate, and the assets are distributed to the intended beneficiaries.

REQUIRED MINIMUM DISTRIBUTION (RMD) – The minimum amount you *must* withdraw from qualified retirement accounts such as a traditional IRA by April 1 following the year you reach age 73.

RISK – The danger or probability of loss.

ROTH IRA – Individual retirement arrangement made with income after the taxes have been paid where designated funds can grow tax-free with no taxes due on the interest earned if the rules for withdrawal are followed.

SEQUENCE RISK – Exposure to an adverse series of negative returns compounded with income withdrawals early in retirement.

TACTICAL STRATEGY – An active investment management strategy for the investor with a shorter timeline that involves the ongoing buying and selling of market investments with the goal of capturing a lower percentage of gains in exchange for a lower percentage of loss.

TRADITIONAL IRA – An individual retirement arrangement that provides a way to set aside money for retirement using contributions that are subtracted from your income (reducing the income taxes owed) and allowed to grow tax-free until the money is withdrawn, at which point taxes are owed on both the principal and interest earned.

TRUST – A legal document used in estate planning that creates an entity separate from you designed to hold the title to assets while following a specific set of instructions for the management and distribution of those assets.

VOLATILITY – A measure of the size and frequency of the change in stock market prices.

WILL – A list of instructions to inform a judge exactly how you would like your estate to be distributed, including your guardian preferences for underaged children.